The Fringe Minority

A Report from the Trenches of the Canadian Freedom Movement

Rick Thomas

The Fringe Minority
A Report from the Trenches of the Canadian Freedom Movement

Copyright © 2022 by Rick Thomas

All rights reserved. No portion of this book may be reproduced in any form without permission from the publisher, except as permitted by international copyright law.

For permissions and enquiries contact:

rick7homas@proton.me

t.me/rick7homas

www.victorycanada.today

"Only through an inner spiritual transformation do we gain the strength to fight vigorously the evils of the world in a humble and loving spirit ... This hour in history needs a dedicated circle of transformed nonconformists ... The saving of our world from pending doom will come, not through the complacent adjustment of the conforming majority, but through the creative maladjustment of a nonconforming minority."

~ Martin Luther King, 1963

Acknowledgements

This record of the first two and a half years of Covid tyranny here in Vancouver, Canada would not have been possible without the enthusiastic and diligent participation, loyalty and devotion of my partner in crime, MB Bose who kept us true to ourselves, dedicated to the movement and focused on freedom.

To all my fellow freedom-loving comrades-in-arms, we salute you for your perseverance under fire. It was you who stood together with us in the rain and snow, week after week, through the lockdowns and Covid insanity. Thank you! You are the best Canadians and you are all heroes! This book is for you.

Contents

Introduction
Chapter 1 How it All Started
Chapter 2 Sovereign Citizens
Chapter 3 Trump Flags
Chapter 4 SueBonnie.ca
Chapter 5 The Vancouver SkyWalkers
Chapter 6 The Truckers' Convoy
Chapter 7 Persecution
Chapter 8 AntiHate
Chapter 9 Division
Chapter 10 Christians & Christ Consciousness
Chapter 11 Scapegoating the Enemy
Chapter 12 Freedom Cells Revisited
Chapter 13 Echo Chambers
Chapter 14 Humans Anonymous
Chapter 15 Fringe Benefits for the Fringe Minority
Epilogue: The Road Ahead

Introduction

"The greatest lie ever told is that vaccines are safe and effective."
~ *Dr. Len Horowitz*

"Vaccination is a barbarous practice and one of the most fatal of all the delusions current in our time. Conscientious objectors should stand alone, if need be, against the whole world, in defense of their conviction."
~ *Mahatma Gandhi*

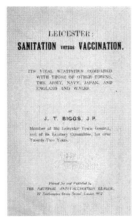

The anti-vaccination movement is not new. It first began in 1840 in England, after the British parliament passed a law mandating compulsory smallpox vaccination for children. In a twist of irony, the inventor of the smallpox vaccine, Edward Jenner, was himself permanently injured as a child, when he was inoculated by variolation, a method used at the time of deliberately infecting someone with pus or dried scabs from an infected person, in order to achieve immunity.

Smallpox is the only disease in the world to be eradicated by vaccination and it took almost 200 years from 1796 when Edward Jenner first tested out his new medical invention on a 14-year old boy. Fast forward to 2022, and we have the World Health Organization promising to rid the world of Covid-19 within a couple years with an untested experimental product.

The very first group to actively oppose mandatory vaccination began in 1866 in Leicester, England, and by 1871, the Anti-Compulsory Vaccination League had 103 branch leagues and claimed 10,000 members.

On November 13, 1919, protesters gathered on the steps of Toronto City Hall to air their discontent with the city's compulsory vaccination program.

In June 1867, an alternative spiritual/holistic health magazine, "Human Nature" campaigned against mandatory vaccinations. It reported that many petitions had been presented to Parliament against compulsory vaccination, and many from parents who alleged that their children had died from vaccinations.

The goal of the Anti-Vaccination League was to "...overthrow this huge piece of physiological absurdity and medical tyranny," quoted Richard Gibbs, who ran the Free Hospital, stating "I believe we have hundreds of cases here, from being poisoned with vaccination, I deem incurable. One member of a family dating syphilitic symptoms from the time of vaccination, when all the other members of the family have been clear. We strongly advise parents to go to prison, rather than submit to have their helpless offspring inoculated with scrofula, syphilis, and mania."

Members of other groups, such as the Church of the Peculiar People, who were conscientious objectors to both world wars, were imprisoned for refusing to vaccinate their children. In Leicester, the number of prosecutions for non-vaccination grew from 2 in 1869 to 1,154 in 1881 and about 3,000 in 1884.

Other more prominent professionals, such as Alfred Wallace, who along with Darwin was the co-discoverer of natural selection, gave evidence before a Royal Commission in 1890, claiming that physicians had a financial interest in promoting vaccination, and that reductions in the incidence of smallpox attributed to vaccination were, in fact, due to better hygiene and improvements in public sanitation.

https://learntherisk.org/vaccines/diseases/

The Anti-Vaccination League published a history of the town of Leicester, who refused to be bullied into mandatory vaccination in 1912. They formed a Sanitation Committee instead and worked diligently to clean up the low standards of hygiene which were normal for that time period.

The Sanitary Committee's head, J. T. Briggs, noticed and demonstrated that when children and adults were vaccinated against smallpox, those who were vaccinated often suffered greater harm or died. Leicester isolated infected individuals and families, and promptly the citizens of Leicester who were infected with smallpox recovered and the disease was contained. The death rate in Leicester fell dramatically with 370 cases – a rate of 20.5 cases per 10,000 of the

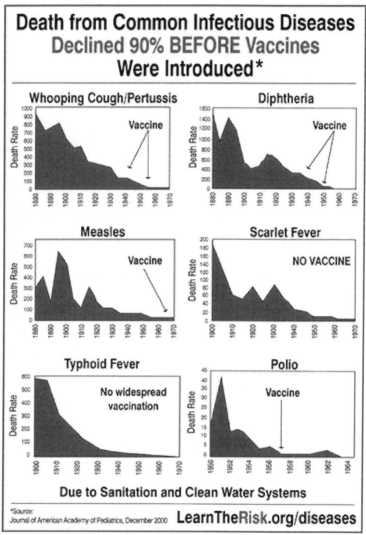

population – resulting in 21 deaths. This was a far lower figure of cases than in some well-vaccinated towns like Warrington (125) and Sheffield (144).

https://www.amazon.ca/Leicester-Sanitation-Versus-Vaccination-Statistics/dp/1528342348

The outcomes were so positive and obvious that the Leicester Anti-Vaccination League lobbied for the law to be changed and in 1898 a new vaccination law was passed in the UK giving conditional exemption of conscientious objectors, the first time "conscientious objection" was recognized in UK law. The moral of the story is that campaigning and social activism against mandatory vaccination works, and governments will back down if enough pressure is applied.

Unfortunately, the world did not learn the lessons the Anti-Vaccination League tried to teach, and from 1990 to 2008, the U.S. Government recorded 238,755 vaccine-related injuries and deaths, according to the VAERS database. Since the FDA estimates that 90% of vaccine reactions go unrecorded, we can extrapolate that during the past 18 years, there have actually been almost 2.4 million vaccine related injuries and deaths!"

To date, the Covid-19 mRNA injections have far surpassed all previous vaccines for injuries and deaths. Data released by government CDC websites, April 3, 2022 point to approximately 69,053 Covid-19 injection related deaths and 10,997,085 injuries for the EU, US and UK combined and these reports are notoriously underreported. The actual numbers are easily ten times these amounts for a conservative estimate.

To date, 66.3% of the world's population has received one dose. If we use the above stats as a gauge, with the total population of 830 million people in the EU, US and UK, extrapolated to the global population of almost 8 billion people, we can estimate that the total adverse events and deaths for the world is approximately 690,000 deaths and 100,000,000 injuries. And that is for a conservative estimate. It is probably closer to 7 million deaths and 1 billion injuries so far if we use the FDA's own estimate that 90% are unreported.

Meanwhile, the scientific community is gradually realizing something is horribly wrong with the vaccines. Over 1000 peer-reviewed papers reveal the mRNA injections are dangerous:

https://www.globalresearch.ca/covid-19-vaccines-scientific-proof-lethality/5767711

Over 17,000 doctors and medical professionals, under the leadership of Dr. Robert Malone, who pioneered the mRNA technology, have signed a declaration that "the state of medical emergency must be lifted, scientific integrity restored, and crimes against humanity addressed."

https://rwmalonemd.substack.com/p/global-covid-summit-declaration-iv

https://childrenshealthdefense.org/defender/nutrition-sanitation-better-than-vaccines-protect-children-from-disease/

The growing avalanche of resistance to the globalists' agenda of world domination is gaining momentum across the world. Our Freedom Movement is just the beginning of the grassroots resistance and the unstoppable revolution that is coming.

This brief effort is not an authoritative history of our movement – historians of the future will no doubt revisit and document the story of our movement, here in Canada, and throughout the world. This is merely one local activist's experience over the course of the first two years of our struggle for human rights, health freedom, justice and the restoration of democracy in the face of medical fascism and government overreach.

If we are to be successful in building a world-wide Freedom Movement, the lessons we learned here in Vancouver are important for our whole movement to take note. We are heading into uncharted waters, the war the elites are waging is unprecedented in human history. Not one of us alone has the clarity or foresight to predict the outcome of the next few years, or even the next few months, but one thing we can say with conviction is that we shall overcome. The battle of all the ages is upon us, guard your hearts well and carry on, brave warriors.

1 / How It All Started

On Tuesday, March 17, 2020, Bonnie Henry, the unelected medical dictator of British Columbia, shut down all schools, nightclubs and restaurants, in a vain attempt to stop the spread of Covid-19. The entire city was a ghost town for weeks, with near-empty streets and closed-down businesses.

NO MORE LOCKDOWNS

GLOBAL MARCH FOR FREEDOM

SUNDAY APRIL 12, 2-5PM

EVERY CITY HALL, VILLAGE PIAZZA OR TOWN HALL IN EVERY COUNTRY: ORGANIZE FRIENDS AND JUST SHOW UP, FILM, MARCH YOUR STREETS & UPLOAD YOUR STORIES BECAUSE THERES MORE OF US THAN THEM!!!

IF YOU SURRENDER YOUR FREEDOMS YOU MAY NOT GET THEM BACK!!!

The emergency declaration gave Provincial Medical Health Officer Dr. Bonnie Henry the ability to be "faster, more streamlined and nimble" in carrying out her directions. Her Royal Highness Bonnie Henry was also authorized to issue verbal orders (royal decrees) "with immediate effect" enabling police officers special powers to carry out those orders. The following day the federal government closed the Canadian borders. At that time, there were only 8 deaths and 596 cases.

On April 12, 2020, after a month of solid lockdown here in Vancouver, a handful of brave men and women stood in front of Vancouver City Hall and protested the government's over-reaching stay-at-home orders.

Independent news journalist, Dan Dicks filmed the event and a 44-second clip of 19 protestors went viral on social media and currently has 3.3 million views. Many of us were at home absent-mindedly scrolling Facebook when we saw the live feed, expecting at any minute to see a paddy wagon roll up to take the "conspiracy theorists" to jail for violating "health orders." But all that happened was public shaming on social media.

https://dailyhive.com/vancouver/coronavirus-deniers-vancouver-protest-video

The event was promoted world-wide and was the first effort to counter the media and government narrative. Judging by the comments on Dan Dicks' twitter feed, the vast majority of Canadians "drank the Koolaid," as Dan pointed out, and sadly, the Koolaid drinkers are completely intoxicated. At the time of this writing, the deaths and adverse effects of the mRNA injections are staggering.

https://www.globalresearch.ca/evidence-millions-deaths-serious-adverse-events-resulting-experimental-covid-19-injections/5763676

Solicitor General Mike Farnworth blasted the "small minority of selfish individuals" in August and enabled police officers to give $2000 fines to event organizers. The Vancouver Police Department refused to give us tickets and VPD Chief Palmer maintained the VPD would respect our right to protest, despite the $531,000 extra policing costs in the first year of the rallies.

https://biv.com/article/2021/08/anti-covid-rallies-put-531000-vancouver-policing-tab

Our Freedom Movement has grown exponentially since those 19 protestors risked it all at City Hall two years ago. We just finished two large rallies at Jack Poole Plaza to protest the Ted Talks event that hosted the notorious Bill Gates, Elon Musk and Al Gore. These two rallies were organized by 20 local groups who all worked together to make the events a big success.

Vancouver hosted Chris Sky several times now at various locations. Some people in our movement say Chris Sky is too rough-around-the-edges and he has a big ego. Maybe this is true, but he has also consistently and openly fought hard for our rights and freedoms here in Canada, at great personal risk and sacrifice. He has been arrested at least 20 times over the last two years, including spending 50 hours in solitary confinement in federal prison. We owe him a debt of gratitude here in Vancouver for his efforts to unite our movement here and get our 20+ groups working together.

No New Normal

No New Normal became the default group that met at the Art Gallery every week for almost 2 years and still continues to meet. It evolved out of the original protest of 19 people at City Hall on April 12th, 2020. Originally the rallies were moved around from  place to place with no fixed schedule which seemed like a better strategy than the unfortunate stagnation that resulted at the Art Gallery protests in the months to come.

The original committee group was called No More Lockdowns, and then briefly Human Rights Movement, which was a better direction for the movement; a more positive statement about what we were fighting for, rather than a negative statement about what we were fighting against.

The leadership at the beginning was dominated by vocal passionate women, many of them moms with young children. Anyone who has studied revolution and civil rights movements is aware that women have played a dominant role in many movements, so it is unsurprising that our movement has followed the pattern of history. The original committee of the Art Gallery protest was about ten people and was soon whittled down to a small handful, for various reasons of personality conflict, internal struggle and diverse political views.

Meeting at the same place, same time every week had some advantages because people could just show up, and the rally did not have to rely on promotion to get people out to the events. On the other hand, it led to stagnation and the weekly rallies degenerated into a social club. Sun Tzu in his classic *The Art of War* advised, "Keep your army continually on the move, and devise unfathomable plans."

Armies are not social clubs and social clubs soon become breeding grounds for gossip, drama and division. We are united by our common goals, not by favoritism, cronyism or group branding. All events, rallies and meetings between freedom people should always have an intention, purpose or goal. Socializing and friendship is the natural byproduct of our involvement with the Freedom movement. We have all made many new friends in the last two years.

The bond of comrades-in-arms is stronger than normal social fraternizing. When we go through things together, working towards higher goals of freedom, democracy, health rights and overcoming tyranny, we become bonded together. People need to know that the other freedom fighters they are working with have their backs in times of crisis.

Many leaders and organizers have come and gone in the last two years. Some shot up like a rocket, and then went straight back down, like one-hit wonders on the pop charts. Others got burnt out or escaped to the B.C. interior, US or Mexico. And new leaders emerged out of the drama created by those who left.

The Freedom Movement is for those who want freedom and are willing to pay the price for it. This may seem like an oversimplification, but the reality is that those of us who are still in the game are fighting for the freedom of all Canadians, even those who are opposed to everything we are doing and saying. They can thank us later, after they wake up.

2 / Sovereign Citizens

At the outset of the pandemic in the early months of 2020, when the whole Vancouver lower mainland was under stay-at-home orders, we joined Kevin Annett's Common Law Assembly group and attended clandestine meetings. The meetings were held in various places, because of prying Karen neighbors, whom we were worried would report us to police. We parked discreetly away from residences and crammed into tiny apartments.

One of the houses we hosted a meeting at was a rooming house. The roommates had a hissy fit when we brought a dozen loud, passionate freedom fighters into the house ranting about Bonnie Henry and Bill Gates. One of them called the landlord who was a lawyer and he appeared at the door the next day to ask that we not hold these meetings because the paranoid Karen roommates said we were "super-spreaders hosting illegal meetings." As it turned out, the lawyer landlord was on our side and told the roommates that the "virus was a hoax." Needless to say, we kept having our meetings there, much to their dismay.

Kevin Annett, at the time, seemed to be the only person in the fledgling movement who had a plan of any kind. With several books under his belt, he had a following and several common law assemblies already up and running, including a 300-member group in Ontario and a national council. At least, that is what Kevin led us to believe.

https://republicofkanata.org/

Annett has a lengthy history of confrontation with the establishment due to his exposing the genocide of indigenous people by Church and State in Canada. Nominated twice for a Nobel Peace Prize and winner of the 2006 award for 'Best Director' at the New York International Independent Film & Video Festival for his grassroots documentary *Unrepentant: Kevin Annett and Canada's Genocide*. A former United Church minister who was kicked out of his church and divorced by his wife for his unpopular opinions, he spent decades in poverty, often living in his car to survive.

www.wikispooks.com/wiki/Kevin_Annett

The common law system Annett devised, made for a 12-person "assembly" that acted as an independent tribunal and home-based cell group. The assembly was sub-divided into three committees of four people each: the legal committees, the education committee and the action committee. It was a simple way to organize a small group of citizens with the goal of activism and social responsibility. After reviewing Kevin's plan of building an alternative society called the Republic of Kanata, the legal team came to the conclusion that his model needed some tweaking.

https://republicofkanata.org/how-does-the-republic-work/

One main point that we agreed on, was not having a public promotion of militias, which we thought was too controversial and risky. We advised changing the word *militia* to *security* in future documents. The other cosmetic suggestions we recommended included upgrading the promotional design, because it was too American conservative and confederate looking.

We presented these ideas to the common law group during the next meeting and this was shared with Kevin, who immediately branded it a "coup" and unceremoniously ousted the four members of the legal team. One of the members sent Kevin a scathing email, accusing him of being a control freak and a tyrant.

Months later, we met Kevin's girl Friday, to learn she had left the Republic of Kanata, and she told us that Kevin's common law assemblies had all fallen apart. Kevin had been existing on donations from members and it was discovered there was no "national council" – it was only a figment of Kevin's imagination.

Organized Pseudo-legal Commercial Argument

The Sovereign Citizen movement may give comfort and solace to those seeking remedy and consolation from that last two years of medical tyranny but the issues with the Sovereign Citizen/Freeman-on-the-Land philosophy are multiple. First of all, it is a movement that lacks credibility with the courts. The Canadian courts have created a policy in dealing with Sovereign Citizens because of a decision by Associate Chief Justice John D. Rooke in 2012.

https://ablawg.ca/2012/10/30/the-organized-pseudolegal-commercial-argument-opca-litigant-case/

Justice Rooke created the collective term "Organized Pseudo-legal Commercial Argument" (OPCA) to describe Sovereign Citizen/Freemen-on-the-Land litigants who attempt to apply "common law" tactics in court.

Justice Rooke's, and by extension, the court's contempt for OPCA litigants is apparent. He characterizes these claims as "pseudo-legal nonsense," "contemptibly stupid," "bluntly idiotic substance," and "byzantine schemes which more closely resemble the plot of a dark fantasy novel than anything else."

The commentary goes on to explain Justice Rooke's conclusions about common law gurus:

"OPCA litigation is apparently a money-making proposition ... the community of individuals he labels "gurus" promote and sell a commercial product in seminars, books, websites, instructional DVDs and other recordings. As Justice Rooke stresses repeatedly the audience for this commercial activity is the client, the potential OPCA litigant, who will be paying for and using the product. Why would people pay for this product? These gurus proclaim they know secret principles and law, hidden from the public but binding on the state, courts, and individuals. Apparently gurus claim that if you use their techniques, you will not have to pay tax or child and spousal support payments; you need not pay attention to traffic laws and will only subject to criminal sanction if you agree to be; you will be able to access secret bank accounts and turn bills into cheques, etc."

Locally, here in the Vancouver area, we watched as yoga studio owner Mak Parhar filed a lawsuit against the BC government, accusing them of kidnapping him and committing terrorism. Mak was part of the Art Gallery protests for months prior to this. He was banned from speaking because he insisted on advocating his Flat Earth ideology, something that is damaging to our movement and makes us look like idiots.

https://www.cbc.ca/news/canada/british-columbia/bc-mak-parhar-lawsuit-dismissed-1.5994166

https://www.bccourts.ca/jdb-txt/sc/21/07/2021BCSC0700.htm

Mak was arrested for refusing to quarantine after returning from a Flat Earth conference in the United States. He also lost his business license for refusing to cancel his yoga classes during the lockdown, a heavy blow for a man with a family.

With all due respect to Mak Parhar, and may he rest in peace, because he was part of our community and he passed away suddenly without explanation. The BC coroner investigated his death, but still no answer to why he suddenly died.

Much of the judgement of Justice Blok mirrors the OPCA ruling of Justice Rooke. He ruled that the lawsuit against the government was "frivolous and vexatious," "embarrassing or scandalous" and "an abuse of process." He also mentioned Christopher James' cases against the Crown which were similarly dismissed.

https://www.canlii.org/en/on/onsc/doc/2021/2021onsc1401/2021onsc1401.html

https://www.canlii.org/en/on/onsc/doc/2021/2021onsc1418/2021onsc1418.html

Many in our movement have gone down the Freeman/Sovereign Citizen rabbit hole, looking for solutions to our current dilemma. The media, our government and health officials are also looking for ways to discredit us and marginalize us from mainstream Canadian society. The average brainwashed Canadian wants to hear that we are a bunch of loonies, because that justifies their compliance and acquiescence.

There is no easy way out of this mess, that can be said without reservation, and perhaps the Sovereign Citizen movement is just one attempt to find an easy way out of our current dilemma.

If the SovCit movement could gain serious numbers in the millions, it might gain credibility, though it would need to be better organized. If the SovCit community could create hundreds, even thousands of Common Law Assemblies, then it would have some legitimacy on the Canadian political stage.

Fringe minorities can become the majority if they are organized, well-funded and have a clear, authentic plan that is practical and easy to duplicate. If you want to abdicate from Canadian society and withdraw from the so-called Corporation of Canada and create your own sovereign independent nation, a nation within a nation, how will it be any different from the one that exists now? How will your education system be any different, how will your police department be any different, how will your economic, political, social system be any different? How do you plan to improve our religious institutions? How do you plan to improve our transportation and communication network? How will it be any different from the existing Canadian society?

3 / Trump Flags

One of the first rallies we attended in early spring of 2020 was held at the False Creek Community Center. People were walking by on the sidewalk calling us racists and homophobes. It was puzzling until we located the cause of the passersby's trepidation: one of the protestors had lined up Trump signs along a fence, facing the sidewalk.

The rallies at the Art Gallery picked up steam and it wasn't long before we had hundreds and sometimes thousands of people at the big events. Much to the dismay of many of us, there were many protestors carrying Trump flags and wearing MAGA hats. Some in our movement, spend more time following American politics, and they want Canada to be a constitutional republic like the United States, with a similar constitution, enshrining gun rights and no universal healthcare.

The Trump lady from the False Creek event had set up a "Trump Shrine," as some of us disparagingly called it. She had arranged numerous posters and banners along a circular bench at the northeast corner of the Art Gallery.

"I love Jesus and I love Trump," she told people.

Vancouver at the time had the lowest support for the American president of any city in Canada. It was around 14% approval rating. The left-wing Vancouverites hated Trump with a passion but the Trump supporters didn't care.

"We're not even Americans," some people groaned.

Then the Trump lady brought her big ass Trump flag onto the steps of the Art Gallery for all to see. There were complaints to the organizers: "She'll drive people away!" Unfortunately, some of the organizers were also Trump supporters, so the pleas landed on deaf ears. One of the leaders, a well-known media personality, climbed on top of the big lion on the side of the steps of the Art Gallery with the microphone in her hand.

"I don't care what anybody says!" she screamed into the microphone. "I love Donald Trump!!"

The crowd responded with a chorus of "Trump! Trump! Trump!"

Operation Warp Speed

And then Trump endorsed, funded and organized Operation Warp Speed. Without rubbing salt on the wounds of his supporters, it needs to be pointed out that a sociopath appears as a savior and then rips you off. That's what they do. Not only did Donald Trump not make America great again, he left it in a far worse condition. The vaccine rollout proceeded full-steam ahead under the Trump administration.

Trump also claimed he took the jab, as well as his wife and daughter. Then he bragged about saving millions of lives: "I think if we didn't come up during the Trump administration with the vaccine, you could have 100 million people dead, just like you had in 1917," Trump said in an interview on Fox News.

https://nypost.com/2021/08/08/donald-trump-says-operation-warp-speed-saved-lives/

Some people in our movement are understandably looking for saviors, especially political saviors. Having said that, it is also admirable that so many people from our movement became candidates, mostly for the PPC party during the last federal election. However, no single person has the political power and influence to win this war for us. We need our combined, collective will power working together to move this mountain into the sea. If anything, we need hundreds and thousands, even millions and billions of saviors, all of them ready to sacrifice everything for the salvation of our planet.

Black Lives Matter

BLM protests were in full gear during the summer of 2020 and the BLM people started showing up to counter-protest our events. The irony of the BLM protestors fighting the system while wearing masks was completely lost on them. The fact that they abandoned social distancing with no increased spread of the virus also escaped their notice, but such is the level of brainwashing in our societies.

There were several altercations with BLM activists that summer. A group of them climbed up the steps onto the stage and a shouting match started between them and a big Russian guy, who disappeared after the incident and never came back. The group of BLM activists were kids really, with skateboards and masks, trying to be cocky and cool, defying their perceived enemy. But we aren't their enemy. The Coke and Pepsi War of American politics has little in common with our Canadian movement for freedom and civil rights.

A few of the BLM girls held up a Black Lives Matter banner on stage right next to our guest speakers. We politely asked them to host their own rally somewhere else. We stressed we were not against them, and we respected their right to peaceful protest, but to no avail. The media did such a great job in labeling us all "far-right extremists," combined with the Trump messaging of our own protestors created enormous opposition from the beginning.

If our movement continues to fight against other civil rights movements, we will gain few allies and create more opposition to our cause. If our movement fights against BLM, LGBTQ, environmentalists, indigenous people, Anti-Asian hate protests, abortion, Islam, legal weed and labor unions, who will stand with us to fight against the New World Order?

4 / The Vancouver SkyWalkers

The Vancouver SkyWalkers is a little known and underrated group that has proven to be one of the most effective and sustained efforts here in Vancouver in reaching out to the normies and recruiting them into our movement.

The Skytrain Conversation Walk began spontaneously last year when a group of mostly young people needed a place to have a meeting and this author volunteered to host the meeting. It was a Friday night, and originally the group leader wanted to get everyone to write letters to their MLA's.

It seemed wishful thinking to try and make a dozen young people sit still long enough to write letters on a Friday night, so it was suggested we make some posters to get the group motivated into doing something practical. The poster making soon evolved into the suggestion to go on the SkyTrain as a protest. They were game and we finished the posters and headed for the train station.

This soon turned into a weekly event that evolved over many months of trial and error, and several brainstorming meetings, before it was refined to where it is today. The reason for its success is half accidental because of the timing of Friday night which is the end of the week and people are finished work, and by 7 pm, they are heading out to visit friends, go out for dinner, a show or the night club.

The SkyTrain also is a closed unit and we have them trapped, and they have nothing to do anyways. On more than one occasion, we were chased away by police. Transit riders often called police when they saw us not wearing masks and carrying posters with provocative writing.

One of our members compiled our experiences and created a manual for the SkyWalkers to follow. It is helpful and instructive to share here in its entirety because it is useful to anyone who is actively trying to reach out to the normies.

(Acknowledgements to Croy Jenkins, with edits for clarity.)

A How To Guide for SkyWalkers

Thank you all for participating within this group. Each of us represents the voice of freedom which speaks against the forces whom seek to destroy our lawfully deserved rights.

As we have rolled into the New Year of 2022, now is the time for us as a society, to become more proficient in our tactics in reaching out to the unaware masses who are oblivious that our inalienable rights as human beings are at stake. These next few months will be critical in gaining ground as the outcome may be decided in spring.

Our Mission Statement:

We are determined in helping citizens by bringing to light information about people's rights and freedoms, lest they be taken away unknowingly.

Our Mantra:

We spread love, not fear. Question, Inform & Connect.

Our Goal:

To spread awareness and plant seeds to passive allies and neutral people in regards to the illegal mandates that have plagued our nation. Gaining numbers of those whom are awake so we can end this Covid tyranny.

Overview:

Together we will go over the following points in an effort to help function as a more cohesive team and share our successes, failures and role plays with each other at the end.

- Why our Method is Successful – Everyone's time matters
- Intent is Fundamental – Keep focused on your goal
- Know Your Target – Be mindful of "sunk time" and "difficulty"
- Vaccines vs. Mandates – Mandates affect EVERYONE
- Facts vs. Feelings – Make it about THEM
- Starting the Conversation – Ask their feelings on current events
- Talking Points – Ask open-ended questions
- Body Language – It's all in their eyes
- Road Blocks – Don't waste time on an opponent
- Closing the Deal – Have handouts ready

Why our Method is Successful:

The key to our team's success at recruiting lays within the psychology behind the location of our team's demonstrations.

Time is the most precious and governing factor for people's lives. It's difficult to explain our message if people feel their time is wasted. (It's important to remember that our time is valuable and limited as well.)

Store Employees & Security Guards are such an example, they are "on the clock" and reaching out to them may prove difficult because we are offering them the dilemma of "our information or your paycheck." They can be won over but the cost of sunk time is too great.

The SkyTrain is most effective because people HAVE time to waste when onboard. They are more willing to hear a freedom fighter speak to them as their personal time is not being infringed upon.

Intent is Fundamental:

When conveying any information to someone, it's integral to keep your intent or goal in the back of your mind. During a conversation, It is easy to get off track, become angry or compromise your position if you lose sight of your intention or goal. Decide on what your goal is before each interaction and focus on what that intention is throughout the conversation, but keep your eyes on the prize.

Check yourself before you wreck yourself: If you notice the conversation has run away from you, it is perfectly OK to take a moment to breathe, remind yourself of your goals and ground yourself before continuing the discussion. The difference between success and failure is the visualization of each step towards your goal or lack thereof.

Know Your Target:

There is a sliding scale in mentality as to how ready people are to receive or engage with the information we have to offer; as such, we have to decide what information to use which would benefit the situation versus losing that person.

(When in doubt, refer to our Mission Statement, Mantra & Goal. Use what works best for you!)

For example, you could explain to someone what graphene is, but because that information could take hours of PowerPoint presentation to convince them, it would yield fruitless in the short amount of time needed to convey that message. While there are many topics one could convey, you will be most successful in choosing a message that the other party can identify with as this will greatly increase your odds of winning them over.

Each person can also be measured within a category of "Sunk Time Cost."

In reference to the images provided, the more people lean on the "opponents" end of the spectrum, the more time, effort and energy it may take to convince them. It's valid to measure your time and effort accordingly, aim for where you feel YOU would be most successful on the barometer. [see image below]

This is a numbers game. For the time it takes you to successfully convey your message to a security guard, you might have used that time to reach 5 "below the nose" mask wearers.

Vaccines vs. Mandates:

While vaccines are a great topic to speak about, many people have either received their 2nd or 3rd shot. As their vaccines cannot be undone, this topic may be unsuccessful with those we speak to; adversely, this might raise their defenses and they may become impossible to reach. Talking about mandates and government overreach may prove more meaningful as it effects everyone equally.

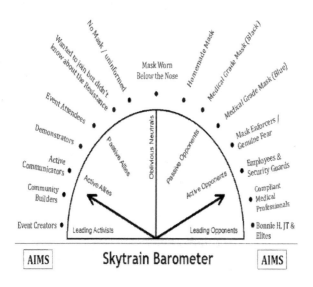

Facts vs. Feelings:

"Facts don't care about your feelings," while true, this statement has never won an argument.

We have reached a new age where feelings are more validated than actual facts and sadly we have to recognize and play by those rules. We can share facts with people whom are willing to accept them but for the most part, people will not do the leg work if we ask them to "Look it up."

This is where the questions which include their feelings on topical matters are effective.

The last 2 years of lock-downs & restrictions were designed to deteriorate one of the most important moral pillars of our society: Community.

If one member of a community faces hardship, the rest of the community will help lift that person up. Without a community, people fall into a paradigm of "If it doesn't affect me, why should I care?"

It's due to this new frame of thought within modern society that we have to direct our questions to "how people feel about the current state of affairs" and "how it directly effects them."

Starting the Conversation:

The best way to start a conversation with someone is to do the following:

- Ask open-ended questions:

Questions that lead to a "Yes" or "No" answer are more likely to kill the conversation. By structuring your questions to be open ended, the other person is forced to think and give an elaborate response.

Ask "how they feel about..." within your question: By asking their feelings on the matter, they will feel more involved as an individual and be more inclined to engage in the discussion.

- Treat everyone as an old friend:

Make the conversation about them and talk to every person you engage with as a friend you've had for a long time. This is an old trick that has gained popularity with motivational speakers. This in effect will make the person whom you're speaking to feel more at ease and cared about, lowering their defenses and more willing to engage.

- Talking Points:

The following are some examples of structured talking points to help further the discussion using the rules applied from above:

- "How do you feel about the restrictions that are in place over the omicron variant?"

- "Do you feel that closing gyms, bars, clubs, with no social gatherings like wedding, dinners, receptions will help limit COVID?"

- "If Omicron offers the same symptoms as the cold and doesn't kill anyone, how do you feel about further restrictions or potential lockdowns?"

- "Do you feel this is still about a deadly virus or more about Government control."

- "Where do we fit in as citizens with rights?"

- "How do you feel about people getting the vaccine, not because they were afraid of a virus, but just so they could enjoy the rights they once used to have?"

- "How long do you feel COVID will go on for? At what point do your rights matter?"

- "If we have another lock down, we could face economic collapse, do you feel you could survive The Next Great Depression?"

Remember, even if your engagement with that person doesn't turn out well, everyone else around is also engaged by proxy. The person you were talking to may not want to take your flyer after the conversation, but another whom was listening in might. This is where it helps to speak to more people at one time – your voice will last longer too!

• Be kind and show love.

"It's easier to catch one fly with a drop of honey than 1000 flies with a gallon of vinegar."

~ Dale Carnegie's: *How to Win Friends and Influence People*

Body Language:

Many people use earphones these days, but if you speak to a larger group of 3-6 whom are sitting down, you may get some heads to look up and maintain eye contact. People may not respond but eye contact is the best indicator to continue your messaging. If you're speaking to a large group of people and they ignore you or if someone feels threatened by your presence, (which they will often tell you to keep away) it would be better to disengage and try again with a different group. Remember that once someone's defenses go up, it will be nearly impossible to reach them and any tactics used on them may be seen as abusive by other passengers which could damage your presentation towards them.

Road Blocks:

There will be times when we are recruiting or demonstrating in public where we are presented with a road block. One such road block is when we encounter a (currently employed) medical field worker. When this happens, you can either ask them questions about their field if you genuinely want to hear their side of the answers, otherwise you are more likely to be successful with your message if you shift the conversation from vaccines to the subject of government over-reach. As far as a medical worker is concerned, they are masters in their field compared to you or what you say. They may not sway even if you quote Dr. Michael Yeadon (Former VP of Pfizer of 30 years), and Dr. Robert Malone (Creator of the mRNA vaccine)

"Never argue with a fool, they will drag you down to their level and beat you with experience."

~ *Letterkenny*

Further talking points to a Medical Worker:

- "How do you feel about the government giving people the ultimatum: Do it or else?"

- "Why is it OK for people to lose their jobs over a government mandated medication?"

- "In what scenario is it OK for people to be denied medical exemption because of their pre-existing conditions?"

- "Do you personally feel there is a line that the government shouldn't cross? What is that line?"

- "Why should someone get vaccinated if you can still catch COVID after having 2 shots and a booster?"

The Fringe Minority

Closing the Deal:

At the end of your discussion, it's imperative to have some information on hand in order to connect them to the awakened world. Information like: Druthers, Pandemic Papers, Common Ground and our group flyers are great resources. Offer them resources that lead to other resources like Telegram groups and other information where their independent exploration can continue. (Be sure to have read the information you're handing out, as a general rule of thumb.)

5 / SueBonnie.ca

No report of our Freedom Movement would be complete without a discussion of Bonnie Henry, the arch-villain of the British Columbia Freedom Movement, and arguably the greatest existential threat to all British Columbians.

Bonnie Henry's status as poster girl for the Covid cult was described in a New York Times article: "It's almost like she was groomed for this time," Dr. Anthony Mounts, a senior advisor for immunizations with the U.S. Agency for International Development, told the NYT. Almost like she was groomed for this time by her handlers, the WHO and the WEF. In fact, she wrote the manual for Canada's Pandemic Preparedness in 2018:

https://www.ncbi.nlm.nih.gov/pmc/articles/PMC5937063/

Bonnie Henry's connection to the WHO is evident. According to her bio: "She worked with the WHO/UNICEF Polio eradication program in

Pakistan in 2000 [which is also funded by Bill Gates and GAVI], and with the World Health Organization to control the Ebola outbreak in Uganda in 2001."

Despite the WHO's claims they have virtually eradicated polio around the world, reports of a hundred cases of a disease "that bears an eerie resemblance to polio" appeared in 2014. In fact, medical professionals are now calling it "Non-Polio Acute Flaccid Paralysis." If it walks like a duck and talks like a duck, then it must be Non-Polio.

A recent Forbes article, dated June 10, 2022, ominously predicts *"There may be a new polio epidemic on its way."*

https://www.forbes.com/sites/williamhaseltine/2022/06/10/there-may-be-a-new-polio-epidemic-on-its-wayif-so-what-we-can-do/?sh=3eea7cc35ebc

https://www.theatlantic.com/health/archive/2014/10/the-mysterious-polio-like-disease-affecting-american-kids/381869/

However, we digress.

Back to Bonnie: There is possibly no other Canadian figure in recent history, other than possibly Terry Fox, who has elicited such an outpouring of devotion. Her cult-like mantra "Be Safe, Be Calm, Be Kind," though appearing to the general public to be inspired by some benevolence and compassion from the goodness of Bonnie's heart, is really just soft fascism. The truth is she is a skillful manipulator who lulled British Columbians into a mind-numbing trance.

People who are afraid and in shock are easy targets for predators. Sociopaths crawl out of the woodwork in times of crisis appearing as saviors. Like all predators, they can smell fear and weakness, and exploit it to the fullest, especially when the crisis is prepared ahead of time with an adjacent plan for corralling the sheep.

CSASPP and the Sue Bonnie Campaign

Early in January 2021, we first noticed a short paragraph online about a software engineer who was planning on launching a lawsuit against Bonnie Henry in BC Supreme Court. The article said he had successfully sued Google for $145,000 and it sounded hopeful and intriguing. We looked up his name online, found his LinkedIn profile and called him.

When we talked to Kip Warner for the first time, it was apparent he was a sharp guy, with a lot of personal discipline – a former army officer with a degree in Artificial Intelligence.

Kip needed $15,000 to start the lawsuit and we hosted a meeting at the local Waves coffee shop and invited a few potential donors. Kip brought his team and they started a GoFundMe campaign soon after the meeting and the necessary money was raised within a week.

Fast forward, over a year and half later and the case has moved towards certification. Kip's legal team has started two petitions as well to challenge the mandatory vaccinations for healthcare workers and the vaccination passports required to enter restaurants, gyms and events.

It is a direct challenge to the emergency measures that resulted in provincial lockdowns, businesses closed, unemployment, bankruptcies and other devastating social ills that occur when a society is under serious stress. The lawsuit already has a 40-day trial set for April 2023. Bonnie Henry will be required to take the stand for seven hours of questioning to explain the science behind her emergency measures.

Parallel to that, CSASPP is petitioning the BC Supreme Court to allow live broadcasting of the 40-day trial. This would be enormous publicity to have it broadcast over the internet all over the world. Reiner Fuellmich is interested in the case and he is planning on attending the trial in person as a consultant. Justice Crerar has called this a "mega-trial" and the largest available courtroom at BC Supreme Court is already booked.

www.suebonnie.ca

Rocco Galati & Action4Canada

The other high-profile lawsuit in the BC Supreme Court, on behalf of Action4Canada who hired Ontario veteran lawyer, Rocco Galati became the great divide in our local movement, something we will touch on later in this book. Suffice it to say, Rocco's challenge is set to be dismissed due to various reasons predicted months ago here:

https://canucklaw.ca/action4canada-statement-of-claim-fatally-defective-will-never-make-it-to-trial/

1. No Concise Set Of Material Facts Provided In Statement Of Claim

2. Section On Relief Sought Is A Complete Mess

3. No Concise Summary Of The Legal Basis For Claim

4. Evidence Being Pleaded In Statement Of Claim

5. Long Quotes Listed In Statement Of Claim

6. Content That Is Unnecessary, Vexatious, Delay Proceedings

7. Proofreading Not Exactly Up To Par

Considering the increasing volume of court cases challenging the health orders, this case is instructive for our movement to learn the basic procedures of a court case. It was revealed in the motion to strike hearing on Tuesday May 31, 2022, that Action4Canada spent $750,000 on the lawsuit. This is from donations within our freedom community.

There are some disconcerting issues with this case that Canuck Law, as well as others, have pointed out. It is painful for our community to sink $750,000 into a lawsuit with zero results. Whatever your opinion of

Rocco Galati and Action4Canada needs to be balanced with achievable results. Otherwise, we will have a difficult time being victorious in our pursuit of restoring our freedom and civil rights.

As a side note, it is a debatable topic whether the Canadian court system and the judges within it are corrupt. We can all agree that our judicial system is not perfect, not always fair and not always efficient. We can also say with some certainty that the judges and lawyers are just as brainwashed as the rest of Canadians who drank the Koolaid and took the jab. The quickest way to wake up the brainwashed judges is to present them the evidence in a court of law, in their arena, in a manner and procedure that they are accustomed to, in a professional manner.

Defamation

On July 14, 2022, Rocco Galati filed a lawsuit against CSASPP for libel and defamation of character for the crime of pointing out his 391-page tome of a filing was vexatious, scandalous and an abuse of process.

https://www.scribd.com/document/582623160/2022-06-28-Statement-of-Claim-Galati-v-CSASPP

And for the second unforgivable sin of allegedly taking part in filing a complaint against Galati with the Law Society of Ontario. Rocco also filed a lawsuit against the Law Society of Ontario:

https://www.scribd.com/document/582623185/2022-07-12-Statement-of-Claim-Galati-v-Law-Society-of-Ontario

6 / The Truckers' Convoy

The Freedom Riders

On May 14, 1961, on Mother's Day, a group of Klansmen, some just coming from church, mobbed a Greyhound bus full of civil rights activists and tossed a firebomb inside. They held the doors shut, intending to roast the activists inside the bus, but fortunately, local police fired warning shots and dispersed the Klansmen.

The thirteen activists, 7 blacks and 6 whites, were part of a coordinated plan of over 300 "Freedom Riders" who planned to ride the racially segregated Greyhound buses from Washington DC through the Jim Crow states of Virginia, South Carolina and Alabama to a rally in New Orleans.

Another of the Freedom Ride buses arrived in Birmingham, Alabama, where it was boarded by

Klansmen, who beat the activists, some of them left unconscious. White activists were beaten especially hard, and one of them, James Peck, required 50 stitches to his head.

For their protection, some of the Freedom Riders were accompanied by state police. They raced with the Greyhound bus at 90 miles an hour to evade snipers and bomb threats all the way from Birmingham to Montgomery. The state troopers abandoned them at the state line and a violent mob entered the bus and beat the activists with baseball bats and iron pipes. White activists again were targeted with extra brutality.

National attention was drawn to their cause and on the following night, May 21, in Montgomery, Martin Luther King gave a speech addressing a crowd of 1500 supporters at a local church. A mob of 3000 local whites surrounded the church, and kept it under siege all night until, at the request of President Kennedy, the National Guard was dispatched to disperse the mob.

Over 300 civil rights protestors were arrested, including several pastors, for violation of segregation laws; many were kept in maximum security prison and denied basic rights; when the Freedom Riders refused to stop singing freedom songs, prison officials took away their mattresses, sheets, and toothbrushes.

Throughout the summer, similar protests were staged and the movement escalated, challenging unjust discriminatory laws. On September 13 of that year, fifteen Episcopal priests including three black priests entered the Jackson, Mississippi Trailways bus terminal coffee shop; they were stopped by two policemen, who asked them to leave. The group refused to leave and all fifteen were arrested and jailed for breach of peace, under a now-repealed section of the Mississippi code that "makes guilty of a misdemeanor anyone who congregates with others in a public place under circumstances such that a breach of the peace may be occasioned thereby, and refuses to move on when ordered to do so by a police officer."

In other words, they were guilty of "being Black in a public place." Interesting to note, the Black Civil Rights movement was also known as the *Freedom Movement*, and for decades the struggle of blacks in the United States was the voice of all humans rights protests. Martin Luther King was not only the spokesperson of blacks yearning for racial equality, he was also the spokesperson of all peoples in all nations who felt the boot of oppression.

Many critics of the our Freedom Movement have disparaged our comparison to the Civil Rights movement in the USA, or our comparison to the mistreatment of the Jews under the Nazi Regime in World War 2. What they are not seeing is the agenda behind the pandemic.

Truckers' Convoy

Fast Forward to January 22, 2022: The Canadian Truckers' Convoy left Prince Rupert heading to Ottawa to protest the unjust vaccine mandates requiring all cross-border truckers to be double-vaccinated with an experimental medical product; a direct violation of medical consent laws and constitutional rights.

Upon arrival on January 29, thousands of peaceful working-class Canadians protested against the Trudeau regime, and the unlawful mandates. The mainstream media launched a full-frontal assault on the truckers, demonizing them with accusations of desecrating statues and making racial slurs at soup kitchen staff.

Objective reporting gave a more balanced view:

https://dailyhive.com/vancouver/ottawa-freedom-convoy-barbecues-bouncy

WEF poster boy, Justin Trudeau claimed, "The small fringe minority of people who are on their way to Ottawa or are holding unacceptable views that they are expressing do not represent the views of Canadians who have been there for each other."

Prime Minister Trudeau's infamous statement sums up the narrative the media are trying to create in the Canadian public's mind. Downplaying the size of the opposition to government's policies is the least of Trudeau's sins. What Trudeau and his World Economic Forum handlers are trying to create is worldwide hatred of the non-conforming, non-vaccinated population, just like the Nazis did by blaming all the woes of Germany on the Jews. And look how that turned out.

Organizers Chris Barber, Tamara Lich and Pat King were arrested on February 17 and 18. Lich's bank account was frozen and many other organizers and donors had their bank accounts frozen. A total of 272 people were arrested and over 2600 fines were given out.

On behalf of downtown Ottawa residents, human rights lawyer Paul Champ filed a $9.8 million class action lawsuit on February 4, 2022, against Chris Barber, Benjamin Ditcher, Tamara Lich, Patrick King and others as organizers of the Freedom Convoy over continuous air horn and train horn noise; a first in Canadian history. Two weeks later, the lawsuit was expanded, seeking a whopping $306 million and the Ontario Superior Court judge ordered $20 million of the money raised to be frozen.

https://www.theglobeandmail.com/canada/article-ontario-court-freezes-millions-in-cash-cryptocurrency-donated-to/

The goon squad was called in after Trudeau used the Emergency Measures Act to stifle dissent and crush the protestors on Parliament Hill. Protestors were abused, beaten, pepper-sprayed and an indigenous woman with a walker was trampled by an RCMP on horseback.

The Rise of Canadianism

"I am a Canadian. Canada has been the inspiration of my life. I have before me as a pillar of fire by night and as a pillar of cloud by day a policy of true Canadianism, of moderation, of conciliation. "

~ *Wilfred Laurier*

The outstanding behavior of the truckers at the Parliament buildings in Ottawa was in marked contrast to the condemning rhetoric of the media and our vainglorious Prime Minister who claimed that "They are extremists who don't believe in science, they're often misogynists, also often racists." The truckers shoveled the sidewalks and cleaned up statues after having been accused of defacing them; there were no violent incidents. They were models of good behavior and yet labeled as violent extremists.

Our own convoy here in Vancouver was an outpouring of exhilarating freedom and "true patriot love" that has never been seen on Canadian soil in our brief 155-year history as a nation. Canadians were never super patriotic like Americans, British, French or Germans. And yet, when the time came, Canadians stood up for their country.

Our Canadian flag is unique in the sea of world national flags. Most national flags are militaristic and project an aura of power and authority. The colorful red and white maple leaf is friendly, optimistic and it has no ego. Canadians do not really have a sense of ethnocentrism and exceptionalism. We are relatively humble, considering we are one of the most influential nations on the world stage. Canadian leaders generally do not project an aura of pride and authoritarianism.

Previous to the Truckers' Convoy, the majority of our Freedom community believed Canadians were asleep, passive and politically apathetic. Many of us repeated the line that Canadians were too compliant and would never rise up. And then the Truckers' Convoy happened, and overnight, Canada became the leader of the worldwide Freedom Movement and all the world's eyes were watching to see what would happen when the convoy hit the streets of Ottawa.

> **Bernie's Tweets**
> @BernieSpofforth · Follow
>
> CANADA - The longest Convoy in the world. Truckers make their way with
> Supporters lining the way, cheering from bridges, delivering food, drinks and buying fuel.
>
> Trudeau has a problem here, a big one.
>
> #TruckersForFreedom #COVID19
>
> 12:12 AM · Jan 26, 2022

And as the saying goes, it's not over until it's over. Pat King is still in jail and Tamara Lich was just re-arrested for breaching her bail conditions. Tyson "Freedom George" Billings was released June 16, after spending 116 days in jail.

We are not conspiracy theorists, extremists, racists, homophobes, anti-semites or misogynists. We are political dissidents, civil rights activists, concerned Canadian citizens from various backgrounds who can see through the clever schemes of the established political hierarchy. The media is not fooling us, the government schills are not fooling us either.

Meanwhile, the Dutch farmers picked up the torch of the Canadian truckers in July 2022, and blocked roads and buildings all over the Netherlands. They even hoisted the Canadian Flag in the square they blocked:

Tamara Lich

Tamara Lich was targeted by the government because she is a threat to Trudeau and the WEF narrative. These comments from former Ft. MacMurray MP Brian Jean are worth reprinting here in full:

"You may disagree with the convoy. You may rightly recognize that some of the people involved in the convoy are distasteful or worse.

You may not like Tamara Lich. She may actually be guilty of counseling mischief – but that hasn't been proven in court. But you should still be worried that

Tamara Lich isn't being treated fairly by the courts. And you have to ask why?

When in Canadian history has anyone been kept in jail indefinitely before a trial for mischief? And in this case, she has only been charged with counseling mischief not actually doing any mischief herself.

Some very nasty, very dangerous people have been released on bail for serious violent offenses. I can't remember seeing a normal person with no criminal background kept in jail pending trial on what are obviously minor charges.

Tamara doesn't own a rig. She doesn't have an air horn to honk. She got a lift to Ottawa with an actual trucker.

She seemed eager to get there to express the frustrations that many Canadians share.

At the beginning of the trip, Lich started a GoFundMe campaign for the convoy. It went viral and it captured the imagination and the donations of more Canadians than donations to any political party in any year.

As near as I can tell, that's Lich's real crime. She is in jail because she became the viral financial symbol of the anger of millions of Canadians.

I don't know Tamara Lich. But I think she is pretty much a normal Albertan. Five foot one. Metis. Motherly and a worry-about-other-people, salt of the earth type. They say she has strong political passions but not much actual political experience or political sophistication.

I have listened to interviews with accountants or lawyers who tried to help some of the normal people involved in the "tiger-by-the-tail" that was the convoy. They make it clear that Lich was working hard to follow the rules on dealing with the money.

By the way, almost none of those millions raised ever got to the truckers, the banks and the government stopped them. All that money is still frozen by a court order. Held for the possible benefit of the people and the lawyers doing a class action suit against the truckers. Lich can't return the money to donors. She can't even use it to defend herself.

How Tamara Lich is being treated is not normal under Canadian law. (THE SAME CAN BE SAID FOR HOW PAT KING IS BEING HELD NOW MORE THAN 120+ DAYS)

Every Canadian should be worried. Worried that someone with no criminal history, who isn't a flight risk, is being kept in jail for minor charges in a non-violent crime, for what appear to be political reasons.

Every Canadian who cares deeply about any political issue should be worried. Every Canadian who might someday have that one protest idea that unexpectedly "goes viral," should be deeply concerned about this very bad precedent."

Pat King Released July 18, 2022 after 150 days in jail with excessive bail restrictions: The judge said King will have to leave Ottawa within 24 hours and also live under a curfew of 10 p.m. to 6 a.m., and he is not allowed to have any involvement in Freedom Convoy activity. He is also banned from social media and forbidden from contacting other convoy organizers including Chris Barber, Benjamin Dichter, Tamara Lich and Tom Marazzo unless in the presence of counsel.

Tamara Lich was released on bail for the second time after Superior Court judge Andrew Goodman overturned a previous decision that sent her back into custody. She had been in custody since June 27, accused of breaching her bail conditions. Judge Goodman said the justice who presided over her hearing made several errors of law and misapprehended some facts when he ordered her continuing detention.

Photo Gallery #1

Courtesy of James Loewen
https://www.facebook.com/james.loewen.75

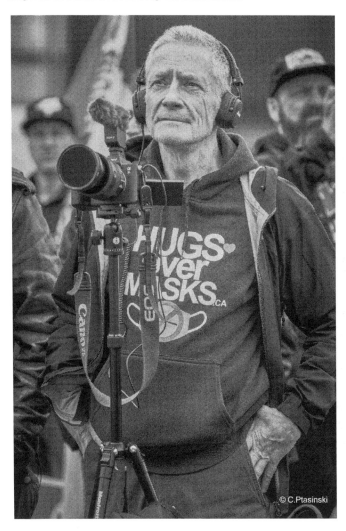

The Fringe Minority

The Fringe Minority

The Fringe Minority

The Fringe Minority

The Fringe Minority

The Fringe Minority

The Fringe Minority

Rick Thomas

The Fringe Minority

The Fringe Minority

The Fringe Minority

Photo Gallery #2 by Chester Ptasinski
https://www.facebook.com/chester.ptasinski

The Fringe Minority

Rick Thomas

The Fringe Minority

7 / **Persecution**

"In a democracy, the majority of the citizens is capable of exercising the most cruel oppressions upon the minority."

~ *Edmund Burke*

Revolutions are typically fought and won by fringe minorities. Prime Minister Trudeau's derogatory remarks reveal that he feels threatened by a small group of vocal opponents. And rightly so, he should feel threatened, because the Fringe Minority is an existential threat, not only to Trudeau's puppet regime, but it is also a direct threat to the survival of the New World Order.

Totalitarian regimes cannot harbor any opposition. They exist by the power of their singularity; a one-eyed, one-party state that acts as all-seeing, all-knowing arbitrator of truth.

Our movement has had its share of critics from the early days, our elected and unelected officials were virtually unanimous in their opposition to any resistance to the Covid narrative.

In one dramatic incident, local comedian/activist, Alex Lasarev was attacked by a man who smashed Alex's van window with a bicycle because he could not bear to hear the contradictory narrative. The man was subsequently charged with assault with a weapon. Telling the truth to brainwashed people is risky, like trying to take a child's security blanket away from them.

https://twitter.com/SkyNews/status/1378312574538719236

On Feb. 23, 2021, a man was assaulted by several Canadian Tire staff for refusing to wear a mask. In the future, a documentary about our movement might be called "Revenge of the Karens." The distorted rhetoric that those opposed to medical tyranny are "aggressive and violent" is in stark contrast to the overt aggression and violence of those who are in agreement with exchanging freedom for "health safety."

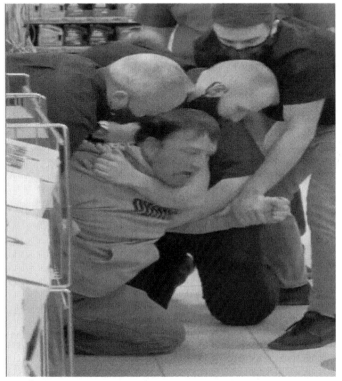

Persecution of minorities is nothing new: The early Christians suffered enormous persecution that also garnered sympathy for their cause, due to the cruelty of the Romans, and the sublime manner that the Christians died. It is a saying in the church that the blood of the martyrs is the seed of the church. Nobody wants to be persecuted, but if you have suffered because of your refusal to wear a mask or take the vaxx, take comfort that it is often through persecution that the greatest victories are won.

Pastor Artur Pawlowski was arrested on Feb 7, 2022 at a peaceful protest at Coutts Border Crossing in Alberta, and charged with mischief over $5,000, and interrupting the operation of essential infrastructure under Alberta's Critical Infrastructure Defense Act. He was held for over 30 days in solitary confinement. Artur explained in an interview with Laura-Lynn Thompson: "I would prefer to be punched in the face than to be kept in isolation. Isolation does such damage to your mind, to your spirit, to your body that you don't know what to do. You want to scream, you want to cry, you want to yell…"

https://www.lauralynn.tv/2022/04/art-pawlowski-is-finally-out-of-jail.html

Pastor Pawlowski was stripped naked multiple times and put inside a metal box with no room to move. He passed out from the heat inside the box, and then he was placed in an extremely cold concrete cell where he lay shivering for hours. Guards incited prisoners to beat him by leaving his cell door open at night.

"Here is the miracle that happened in prison," he described the daily vigil conducted by his family outside the prison walls who prayed for him. "Those boys are alone, no one cares for them."

He spent his free time praying and encouraging the prisoners. Many came to see him and he started a Bible Study and a church service in the prison. By the time he was released, his entire unit was participating in the Bible Study, with even Muslims, bank robbers and murderers attending. One of the prisoners thanked him saying, "You have restored my faith in humanity." There is always good news, if you believe in good news; there is always a silver lining to every dark cloud: *"Happy are they who are persecuted for righteousness' sake, for theirs is the kingdom of heaven. Happy are you when men shall revile you and persecute you and shall say all manner of evil against you falsely. Rejoice and be exceedingly glad, for great is your reward in heaven."*

On Friday, July 22, 2022, Alberta's Court of Appeals ruled that the injunction was "not sufficiently clear and unambiguous," meaning the Pawlowski brothers contempt of it must be "set aside." The panel also ordered that the fines the Pawlowskis paid be reimbursed, and that the Pawlowskis' costs, set at $15,733.50, be paid by Alberta Health Services to the brothers. They added that because the contempt findings were dismissed, "the sanction order must also fall," referring to the punishments the Pawlowskis faced as a result of their alleged contempt. Another win for the Freedom Team.

Chris Sky and his wife, Jenny, arrested at West Edmonton Mall, Nov. 18, 2021 for not wearing masks. Chris and his wife had all charges dismissed July 8, 2022

Dr Mel Bruchet Wrongfully Confined in Psych Ward

In late December of 2021, a retired North Vancouver physician, Dr Mel Bruchet began speaking out publicly concerning the sudden rash of infant deaths at Vancouver Children's Hospital, and committing the unforgivable sin of tying these deaths to mRNA injections, taken by the babies' pregnant mothers.

His activism led to a series of rallies in front of the RCMP station, adjacent to Lion's Gate Hospital. Confrontations with police escalated to his dramatic arrest at his home witnessed by Dr Hoffe and Dr Nagase. Eight police officers in two squad cars were dispatched to apprehend an 80 year-old man.

Dr Mel was taken in handcuffs to the misnamed Hope Psychiatric Center where he was drugged and denied basic rights such as telephone calls and visitors. He was given anti-psychotic medications which are not prescribed to elderly people because it gives them strokes and heart attacks, and unsurprisingly, he had two mini-strokes. He was put through mental health kangaroo courts accusing him of thought-crimes about the Covid vaccines that the institutional quacks labeled as "delusions," evidence of his "dementia or psychosis."

After many failed attempts by supporters, friends and fellow activists to have Dr Mel released, he was luckily given a day pass, and he escaped. Dr Mel was forced to go into hiding for weeks because the RCMP put a warrant out for his arrest. This is the New Normal. If they can do it to him, they can do it to any of us.

Dan Dicks Wins in Court

On Friday September 10th 2021 Dan Dicks called the Pacific Gateway Hotel in Richmond to ask if it was now a current quarantine facility to which the reply was "no comment"…after visiting the hotel and speaking with the manager Dan was also given no answer and was asked to wait for the right person to come. Not long after, the police arrived and Dan and his wife were subsequently detained and fined $1000 each for "breaching a quarantine facility." Dan won his day in court July, 2022.

https://pressfortruth.ca/the-truth-has-prevailed-press-for-truth-1-bc-courts-0/

8 / AntiHate

Much of the intel being collected against the Canadian Freedom Movement is happening online on Twitter feeds of the AntiHate.ca organization that is funded by the Canadian government's *Anti-racism Action Program* www.canada.ca/en/canadian-heritage/services/funding/anti-racism-action-program.html

Their mandate, according to their website:

"The Canadian Anti-Hate Network counters, monitors, and exposes hate promoting movements, groups, and individuals in Canada using every reasonable, legal, and ethical tool at our disposal."

Their Twitter feed @antihateca claims they are "Fully independent and nonpartisan" despite government funding and blatant left-wing ideology and anti-conservative bias. They assume a high moral stance by profiling and documenting racism in Canada, but in reality, AntiHate.ca is more accurately described as Anti-right.

All the outspoken critics of the Freedom Movement, whether it is Trudeau or Global News, play the race card. AntiHate has only race cards in its deck and they are consumed with the singular narrative that any conservative (or white person) is automatically a racist. It is a clever game to play, pretending to fight the unforgivable sin of racism and assuming the role of Anti-racist Grand Inquisitor.

Although, eradicating racism from society is a noble undertaking, it is also arguably impossible and naive to attempt to stomp it out via Tweets on social media. The same could be said for any human failing, such as addiction or domestic abuse. The "Just Say No To Drugs" campaign failed, so why would they think their Just Say No To Hate campaign could be any more successful? Taking the moral high ground safeguards them against any accusation of hatred or racism, though it is apparent they vehemently despise the conservative right of Canada, in all its forms and varieties.

There are several Twitter accounts associated with this group but a couple of the main ones are Drew @nolifeneet and Kurt Phillips @ARCCollective who are both board members of AntiHate.ca. These accounts have trolled our movement from day one with massive tweets, especially from @nolifeneet who is most likely AntiHate executive director Evan Balgord. His Twitter account is over 30K tweets, indicative of a full-time paid social media hack. (Others include @JaneQCitizen @HugsMasks @MackLamoureux @BernieFarber @YYCantiracist @VestsCanada)

Balgord is also a board member of an organization that exists for the sole purpose of pushing Facebook to increase censorship in the name of democracy. "As Meta shareholders meet to discuss the future of the company, their platforms continue to do active harm to civil rights, human rights, public health, and democracy worldwide. In spite of knowing how to turn off the flow of hateful, inflammatory, and misleading content on Facebook, they won't do it, because the profits are too great."

https://rfob.medium.com/real-facebook-oversight-board-joins-national-effort-to-demand-corporate-governance-reforms-at-meta-220a76694e02

Rick Thomas

As a disclaimer: all political movements have fringe people who may or may not represent the best interests or the ideology of the core group. The assumption of AntiHate and the rest of the Antifa groups is that if there is one racist in the group then they must all be racists. This is poor logic. There are Buddhists in our movement. Does that mean we are all Buddhists? There are New Agers in our movement. Does that mean we are all New Agers? The Canadian Freedom Movement represents a broad cross-section of Canadian culture and AntiHate.ca commits the crime of deflecting from the real issues of civil rights and freedoms, vaccine injuries, government over-reach, medical tyranny and corporate greed.

The careers section of AntiHate is particularly revealing: Jobs pay $55K for investigator (inquisitor) or researcher (propagandist) and the applicant must be anti-racist (holy) and anti-fascist (self-righteous) in order to be effective at rooting out the racists (heretics). Applicants must also demonstrate that they "… are capable of pseudonymously joining hate groups/channels/chats … to expose far-right and white supremacist movements." And again, considering the broad scope of the accusatory online rhetoric of the AntiHate staff, the implied subtext is that all right-wingers are white supremacists.

https://www.antihate.ca/careers

Does this group compile and report their findings to the Canadian government, RCMP and CSIS? Your guess is as good as mine.

And speaking of CSIS:

CSIS has been monitoring our movement, specifically the Ottawa Freedom Convoy: David Vigneault, director of the Canadian Security Intelligence Service (CSIS), recently said "We have seen a number of individuals, who were of concern to CSIS prior to the convoy, being engaged online and also in person in the context of the convoy." Vigneault testified before a special joint committee investigating the invocation of the Emergencies Act in February, in response to the convoy occupation of the Parliament buildings area.

"The concern we had with the convoy, at the outset and throughout, was the fact that we have seen in Canada, in other jurisdictions, violent extremists using these protests and demonstrations to engage in acts of violence, to recruit members, to be able to spread their ideology further." CSIS was also concerned about the risk of lone actors, who would "be engaged in violence spontaneously," Vigneault said.

As cited by The Guardian, the CSIS division of the Integrated Terrorism Assessment Centre (ITAC) report said supporters of the convoy "advocated civil war," called for violence against Prime Minister Justin Trudeau, and said the protest should be "used as Canada's January 6," which is a reference to the storming of the United States Capitol in Washington DC in early January last year.

"Extremists and other individuals supporting Covid-19 conspiracy theories and violent anti-authority/anti-government views have expressed intent to participate in the convoy and to attend the accompanying protest in Ottawa," The Guardian said, quoting from the ITAC report.

The worst violence at the Ottawa Convoy protest was probably a snowball fight, but we are dealing with government spy agencies who need to justify their jobs with outlandish claims and exaggerated reports. Any government hack knows the best way to keep your job is by telling the government what it wants to hear.

https://www.lavalnews.ca/freedom-convoy-2022-advocated-civil-war-csis-intel-report-claims/

Another thing to keep in mind, the entire country was under lockdown mandates for months, and this meant that CSIS and ITAC were also forced to stay-at-home and work remotely which drove them all into online investigation.

The tactics of the federal government towards freedom activists has been intimidation, public slandering and jail. At the time of this writing Pat King is still in jail on a range of charges. Meanwhile, he has very little support from the Freedom Movement and some have called him out on social media, claiming he is "selling out" by brokering a plea deal. Easy to say when you are sitting at home behind your laptop, and not sitting in jail for days on end, facing ten years in federal prison.

Stomping out the Nazis in Canada is an admirable pursuit. However, the Anti-Hate group have far exceeded their mandate of nonpartisan, anti-fascism and anti-Nazism, expanding their sphere of influence into the entire conservative political arena. A truly non-partisan effort would be fighting racism, bigotry and hate on both sides of the political fence. It is epic hubris and political ethnocentrism to believe your side of the political spectrum is above reproach, and without sin.

Ironically, Vladimir Putin and the Russian military, in the Ukraine, are attempting to stomp out real Nazi brigades, not just wannabe Nazis who read David Duke and think they are enlightened. And these same so-called anti-Fascists are openly supporting the pro-Nazi Ukrainian government.

There is much confusion about who our real enemies are at the moment because of the pandemic which has blinded and confused the whole world. The truth is that the left and the right have the same enemy. The New World Order hates all of us, no matter which side of the political fence we are on.

Hatepedia

The latest entry in government-funded citizens' inquisition groups, Hatepedia.ca, rolled out its list of obscure and virtually unknown Neo-Nazis that are supposedly taking over the country, even though they are so obscure and virtually unknown that they probably have about as much impact as a mosquito on a rhinoceros' back.

The project was given a $340,000 grant from the Government of Canada's Anti-Racism Action Program to fund the 18-month program. Online Hate Research and Education Project (OHREP), of which Hatepedia is the cornerstone. "OHREP explores how memes and other digital practices are being used to spread hatred in Canadian contexts…"

www.hatepedia.ca

The Canadian Anti-Hate network is, in reality, a Hate-Canadians Network who have become the thing they hate. They are bigots, plain and simple, who hate working class Canadians, especially rural Canadians. They are young urban professionals who cannot tolerate the agricultural backbone of our country. Nor do they tolerate the values of rural, conservative Canadians.

In the 2019 election, it was apparent the divide in Canada is along rural/urban lines: "The Conservatives won 121 ridings with an average density of 423 people per square kilometer. That compares with an average density of more than 2,000 people per square kilometer in the 157 Liberal-held seats and almost 1,900 in the 24 NDP seats. (The national average density per riding is 1,418.)"

https://www.nationalobserver.com/2019/11/05/analysis/density-matters-clear-divide-between-urban-and-rural-canadian-voters

https://globalnews.ca/news/8220649/canada-election-results-urban-rural-divide/

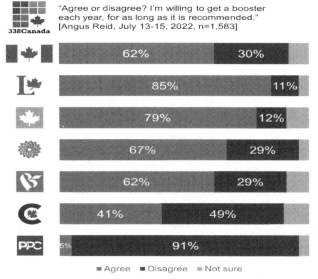

One of the most revealing surveys from June 2022, polled 1500 Canadians, and a whopping 44% (the equivalent of 13 million Canadians) believe "big events like wars, recessions and the outcomes of elections are controlled by small groups of people working in secret against us," and almost as many agree "much of our lives are being controlled by plots hatched in secret places."

The bias of the survey company, Abacus Data, is apparent when they moan, "Perhaps the most disconcerting thing in these numbers is the fact that mistrust of institutional accounts isn't simply neutral skepticism – it is often accompanied by a willingness to believe dangerous contrarian theories. This threatens to undermine the ability of political parties, businesses, civil society groups, and governments to help build consensus and make progress together."

BIG EVENTS LIKE WARS, RECESSIONS, OUTCOMES OF ELECTIONS ARE CONTROLLED BY SMALL GROUPS OF PEOPLE WORKING IN SECRET AGAINST THE REST OF US

	AGREE	DISAGREE
NATIONAL	44%	56%
PPC VOTER	77%	23%
CPC VOTER	51%	49%
GPC VOTER	39%	61%
NDP VOTER	39%	61%
LPC VOTER	40%	60%
TRUST GOV'T ACCOUNTS	65%	35%
DON'T TRUST MEDIA	68%	32%
NO COVID SHOTS	73%	27%
LEFT	35%	65%
CENTRE	46%	54%
RIGHT	50%	50%
IDENTIFY W POILIEVRE	56%	44%
IDENTIFY W CHAREST	32%	68%

TRUST AND BELIEFS IN CANADA 2022

The New Democracy is now an integral part of the New Normal: a revisionist democracy where freedom of speech means having only one viewpoint expressed, in order to "help build consensus and make progress together." Any other voices are seen as "dangerous contrarian theories."

The average urban Canadian has taken a deep dive into the abyss of totalitarianism, and yet believes that they are achieving some kind of progress. If progress means blindly supporting a fascist medical state, then it is better to stagnate. In our strange new Orwellian reality, there is no longer any love, there is only hate and anti-hate.

9 / Division

"When there is no enemy within, the enemies outside cannot hurt you."

~ *Winston S. Churchill*

Every single leader in the Vancouver area, including this author, has been accused at one time or another of being controlled opposition. It is a repeated pattern that whenever leaders and organizers get into conflict or they have disputes with each other, they are invariably accused of being paid infiltrators sent in by CSIS, the Illuminati or whoever to disrupt and divide our movement.

The experience over the last two years points to the uncomfortable conclusion that we don't need any help in dividing ourselves, and there are a variety of reasons for this.

For starters, there are a mixed bag of political worldviews in the movement; although we are dominated by conservatives we are not all conservatives – there are many liberals, libertarians, anarchists, vegans, socialists, centrists, indigenous, environmentalists, New Agers and others in our movement that creates a potential staging ground for conflict and differences of opinion.

Combined with this is the awkward truth that we live in a dysfunctional society with decades of family breakdown. We would be naive and unrealistic to think our Freedom Movement does not have dysfunctional and broken people within its membership, even among its leaders.

Healthy competition between leaders is desirable and as long as the competition is friendly, and good sportsmanship conduct is maintained, then it contributes to the growth of the movement. People, being human and fallible are often unconsciously motivated and emotionally charged by jealousy, competition, ambition, vanity, and need for recognition and approval by others, but when competition turns into vicious infighting and drama, it affects everyone, and over the last two years, even our enemies could not help but notice the division in Vancouver:

Drew
@nolifeneet

No anti-lockdown activist community has infighting like the Vancouver area's does.

How do we as a Freedom movement stay united when there are so many divergent forces pulling us apart? And inside our own movement we have division, drama, debate and separation.

Despite the rhetoric from our nefarious prime minister, we are not a homogenous blob of extremists, misogynist racists and homophobes. The truth is we are a mixed bag of different groups who have been all thrown together by our common refusal to take an experimental mRNA injection. There are also vaccinated people joining our ranks after waking up the hard way, some from vaccine injuries and others, after realizing that the mandates still stuck and life didn't get back to normal.

We need to remember that we are a human rights movement, first and foremost. Secondly, we are a healthcare movement and thirdly, we are a spiritual movement. If we can focus on these three things, we will stay strong and united. When we get sidetracked into other areas, we start to get lost.

One of the most difficult things that all of us have to be aware of, and actively do, is to put aside our political and religious beliefs for the time being. This is very difficult when we are being inspired and motivated by these same political and religious beliefs. Many of the events, rallies and freedom circles have turned into a Sunday service when overzealous Christians lead them. It is not hard to see things from their point of view: Should a Christian stop being a Christian? Should they be silent when they see something that doesn't jive with their worldview?

There is also a high percentage of New Age people within our movement who are spiritual but not part of a religious organization. They do not embrace a monotheistic worldview nor are they inspired by the Abrahamic religions.

Some people in our movement are more inspired by Eastern religions and achieving higher states of consciousness and reaching the fifth dimension. They are concerned with mindfulness and believe we are immortal eternal beings living in a physical body experiencing an earthly existence.

There are also many alternative health practitioners and followers of naturopathic medicine who practice Reiki, yoga and energy healing that is in sharp contrast to Western pharmaceutical medicine.

Though it is not necessary to give up our core principles in order to appease others who have different world views, it is also important that we try to embrace everyone's world views without committing to any of them. We can adopt a position of wanting to win everyone over to our cause without feeling obligated to join or agree with everything.

This is a bit of a juggling act and walking a fine line but there are many people within our movement who are able to do it. Some, unfortunately, are not able to do it and either split off from those with differing world views or push them away.

We have witnessed several divisions within our movement when groups split in half over different issues. Though the issues in each division were different, the common theme that always emerges is the egos of the leaders.

Ego is ultimately divisive but selfless service to others unites. There may never come a time when we will achieve such a level of unity that we have no difference of opinion with anyone. This seems naive to believe that, at least here on this physical reality, on this planet Earth, at this time.

Over the last two years many leaders have come and gone but a common theme is that the humble leaders that really want to serve the Freedom Movement keep rising to the top and the ones with egos are ending up being left behind because it becomes obvious to everyone the degree of their self-interest and self-absorption.

Ultimately, at the root of our movement we need to be motivated by a selfless desire to heal our nations and restore our civil rights and freedoms. We must be inspired by a vision of the future that we can achieve, and build a much better society than the one that created the mess that we currently find ourselves.

When selfish people fall upon the rock of selfless service their fragile egos becomes crushed and those that throw themselves into the Freedom Movement wholeheartedly relinquish their egos or allow their egos to be disintegrated by the greater cause we are confronted with.

To make a long story short, how do we stop division from happening? The answer is we can't. We must embrace division and realize that sometimes division is better than staying together with people who have different ideas and different directions. It is very painful for groups that have worked together so long to separate, like getting a divorce. There are often a lot of mud slinging and accusations thrown around. The secret is to divide without breaking fellowship with people, just like when people get divorced sometimes it's very messy, and other couples are able to maintain an amiable divorce. We can mutually decide to go our own ways and still remain friends and Freedom fighters and brothers and sisters in arms.

Branding

There was much concern about group branding in the first year. Many people wanted us to stay a big, happy family with no logos or organizations displayed on tents at the rallies. Some complained about the logos on the posters promoting upcoming events. They felt this was mirroring the corporate world of brand-names, copyrights and trademarks; the very same corporate world we are fighting against.

And still others, felt the brand names advertised by the emerging groups was just ego and self-promotion, and we should just have a generic freedom movement without breaking off into different groups; a no-name brand freedom movement.

All of the above are valid criticism because we all witnessed leaders' personal attachment to their own brand, even to the point where it sometimes became apparent that fighting for freedom was secondary for certain leaders, and the main goal was playing the fame game of popularity.

There has been more than one leader who encountered their first taste of fame and popularity in the movement, a powerful drug for some people. Being on stage and addressing large crowds of hundreds, and even thousands of people is an intoxicating feeling for people with an inner need for recognition and praise.

Leaders' egos can indeed become entangled in their group and the group can become "my baby" if people are not careful to avoid possessiveness of their group.

One of the groups we were involved with split in half because of the desire of some who wanted to change the name of the group to something more positive. This created much unnecessary social drama. Some of the members were emotionally attached to the name and the feeling of security the group provided with weekly meetings.

It is true this is a trying, difficult time and we all need moral support, some more than others. The rallies, events, organizations and groups can become security blankets for anxious and lonely people in the movement.

Ownership

Ownership is a double-edged sword and it can lead to both positive and negative outcomes: Freedom fighters may exhibit exemplary citizenship behavior like the truckers did in Ottawa. Many devoted people in the movement have given much personal sacrifice, including losing jobs, friends and family. Others mature and take on extra responsibility and stewardship.

There are also negative outcomes, especially when that sense of ownership is challenged and people experience feelings of personal loss or there is major social drama as we have experienced. Our community is dominated by an older demographic, and often older people resist change and are unwilling to accept advice because they are too set in their ways.

McFreedom

The truth is there are no "owners" in the Freedom Movement. The groups that have sprung up are almost all unincorporated, non-legal entities, run by ad hoc committees. You cannot trademark freedom or operate events and rallies like a McDonald's franchise. Many people in the movement aspire to leadership positions but true leadership is about service not about lording it over others. Whoever wants to be leader should want to be everybody's servant.

We do not want or need a giant umbrella group that overseas our whole movement. It would be too difficult to maintain and we would run the risk of being infiltrated. We are far better off to form hundreds and thousands of small groups and work to unite them all as best as we can in our local area. Each group can interact and connect with as many small groups as possible and we can create a giant interconnected web of Freedom cells and organizations.

Conservatives and Liberals

Although much of our movement is dominated by conservatives, are the conservatives willing to put aside their political differences for the sake of our movement? Because much of the brainwashed people we are trying to wake up are on the left of the political spectrum, and it is very difficult for us to reach out to them in a meaningful way if we are still in a political war with them.

Winning the left over is an epic challenge. Many people on both sides of the political spectrum have been born into conservative or liberal families and have been conservatives or liberals their whole lives. We cannot escape the fact that there are many libertarians in our movement and increasingly, more labor union people are joining our movement because their unions failed them, especially the healthcare workers who were betrayed by their unions and fired for not taking the experimental mRNA injection.

Workers' Revolution

Our movement needs to build bridges with union members and unions leaders. The majority of those affected by the lockdown measures and vaccine mandates have been the working class who have suffered the brunt of the economic pain of the last two years. The so-called Fringe Minority is in fact, the Fringe Majority.

The truckers' convoy in Canada is a perfect example. Between 12,000 and 16,000 truckers were put out of work because of the vaccine mandates required to cross the Canadian US border. These truckers are part of the backbone of our society.

Most people in our movement are diametrically opposed to Marxism, and though, none of us want to be thrown into a totalitarian communist police state such as the 62-years of Soviet control in the USSR, what we really need is a worker's revolution.

Can the conservatives in our movement pick up the torch that the left has dropped and speak for workers and labor unions all over the world without descending into Marxism and socialism?

10 / Christians & Christ Consciousness

"Let us meditate until we perceive the Infinite Christ reigning in our own hearts. Let us learn to love those who love us not; and to forgive those who do ill against us. Let us break all our mental boundaries of color, creed, and nationality, and receive all – even our inanimate and animal brothers – in the endless, all embracing arms of our Christ Consciousness. This will be a true and fitting celebration of the coming of Jesus Christ to this earth."

~ Paramahansa Yogananda

At the risk of creating division, it is an observation that there are a couple spiritual groups within the Freedom movement that stand out. One is the Christian community and the other is the New Age community. Christianity is one of the pillars of our western civilization, the other pillars being Roman law and administration, and Greek art and philosophy. The New Age movement has gathered strength over several decades, having its roots in the late 1800's, when many North Americans became disillusioned and disenchanted with Christianity.

Any spiritual path can become a vice, instead of a virtue, and anything can be made an idol. Spiritual people, throughout history have chased after false gods and false messiahs primarily due to a lack of discernment. A society's inability to discern the difference between a saint and a sociopath may coincide with the unintended consequences of civil unrest and totalitarian regimes.

We can all be guided, if we are seeking Source and have the courage to follow the guidance of the Source. Any religion or spiritual path can be selfish if you're only concerned with your own salvation and your own enlightenment. True religion and true spirituality are based on the individual believer's experience pursuing the Source of the universe, and becoming less self-centered and more universe-centered and more Source-centered in the process. The quickest way to achieve this is by serving others. Nothing gets you off your own self and your own issues faster than helping someone else or doing something positive for the greater good. And it is through service to others that we grow the most.

Our movement is a macrocosm and a testing ground for do-gooders who care enough about our broken world to give up their own lives in order to fight tyranny and create a better world.

The self-help tradition of the New Age movement can be just as self-serving and hedonistic if the goal is just personal gratification and self-enhancement. The Freedom Movement is a testing ground for many activists because we are all required to be humble, give up our egos in order to serve the greater good of the Movement, resist tyranny and create a new society based on better values and ideals.

You cannot win the fight for freedom if your ideal of freedom is not better than the ideal of your enemies. Unless we create a Greater Reset than what the WEF is offering we cannot hope to win over our fellow citizens.

Unity Not Uniformity

Once we realize that we are not united by the things we agree on, we can begin to achieve unity. We are united by our common goal(s) and our common spiritual destiny and our common spiritual Creator. We do not need to make our members all think the same. There will always be disagreement between us because we are a mixed bag of Canadians with differing backgrounds, perspectives and attitudes.

We can be united by our common spirituality as long as people in our movement recognize that there are people of multiple religious and spiritual backgrounds. We all need to be inclusive whenever possible. This isn't a Christian Movement or a Conservative Movement or a New Age Movement. It is a civil rights movement. If we fight for freedom of speech we are fighting for freedom of speech for all Canadians, not just our private interest group.

Religious Tolerance

Our Canadian Charter of Rights states we have the right to worship in whatever manner we want without interference from the government. Religious rights are based on the idea of religious tolerance. It does not hurt you if someone is Muslim, Christian, Hindu, Sikh or Jew.

We are fighting for freedom of speech for everyone and freedom of worship for everyone, not just for our own special interest group. If we deny and exclude others' style of worship or worldview we are denying their rights and freedoms.

This is a challenge for all religious people to be able to embrace other religious beliefs without committing to them. Many people are disaffected or negatively impacted by Christianity, while others within our movement feel their religion is the only way, and therefore they have an urgent imperative to tell others how it is. Can we reconcile all the different views within our movement? The answer is probably not. Neither is it possible for all religions on the Earth to merge into one. There are just too many obstacles and differing religious beliefs to make that happen.

Another thing to note is that this is a global problem. Practically all countries in the world have signed up for the WHO pandemic restrictions; even Middle Eastern countries that are Muslim and India which has a large Sikh and Hindu population; and therefore our global international fight is for freedom of religion for all people and freedom of speech for all nations.

Christianity is actually ideally situated to be the unifier of our Freedom Movement, if Christians can get past the theological box that many seem to create around themselves. Jesus of Nazareth tore down barriers and broke traditions and customs in order to reach people. One of the biggest issues for Christians is tolerance and it seems Christianity has not been a very tolerant religion throughout its history, but maybe that needs to change.

Christian churches are already being used by our Movement for weekly events and organizations. Churches already have the buildings and the structure in local communities all over the Western world and in many parts of Africa, Asia, South America, and even into the Middle East. This may indeed be a rare opportunity for Christianity to let go of its need for dominance and religious superiority, and humble itself at the foot of the cross, like its leader did, and truly become a servant, not only to our Freedom Movement but to the rest of the world.

Are Christians up for this monumental task? Because if they drop the torch, someone else will pick it up and become the torch bearer to bring us into a true new age of democracy, freedom, civil rights, and spiritual revival.

The New Agers also have the same opportunity to unite our Movement. Many of the natural health professionals seem more inspired by Eastern religion than by Western religion. Will this opportunity to bridge the gap between the East and the West be taken advantage of by spiritual people in our freedom community?

Can Christians learn from the New Agers? Are they open to new ideas of healing and medicine such as Reiki, yoga and crystal therapy? And conversely can the New Agers and natural health practitioners learn from the Judeo-Christian tradition that Western society has built much of our values upon? Can spiritual people within our Movement bridge the gap between Sikhs, Hindus, Buddhists and Muslims here in Canada and elsewhere in the world?

11 / Scapegoating the Enemy

Our Freedom-loving crew are unanimous in believing that a cabal of super-wealthy, powerful (mostly) men have taken over practically all institutions in our societies. We also agree they are sociopaths with a far-reaching agenda for global domination.

We're not quite so unanimous, however, about the identity of these people, and during the last two years, in the trenches of the Freedom Movement, there have been all kinds of theories about who sits at the top of the pyramid and who is responsible for all-the-evil-in-the-world. A short list would include:

Satan
Jews / Zionists
The Vatican / the Pope
Aliens
NASA
Liberals
Communism / Socialism
Feminism
LGBTQ
The British Empire
British monarchy
China

However, here are some of the things that are rarely mentioned as the cause behind our global malaise:

The Sacred Cow

Very few mention capitalism, for starters. Generally, capitalism is a sacred cow within our movement, somehow it is pure and holy, and not the cause of any global problems. Most will claim the capitalism practiced by the bankers, weapons manufacturers, corporate owners, hedge fund owners, oil company executives, media moguls is not "true capitalism."

Many in our movement are small business owners who are threatened by the heavy-hand of the state upon their right to make a living as guaranteed by our Charter of Rights, section 6:

> (2) Every citizen of Canada and every person who has the status of a permanent resident of Canada has the right:
>
> a) to move to and take up residence in any province; and
>
> b) to pursue the gaining of a livelihood in any province.

It does not make anyone a communist for pointing out that the people and institutions behind the pandemic are all hardcore capitalists like Bill Gates and the Rockefeller Foundation, Klaus Schwab and the World Economic Forum. Bill Gates monopolized the PC market through ruthless destruction of the competition. He was found guilty in 1998 of violating anti-trust laws in his blatant attempt to corner the PC market. Gates' evasive rhetoric during the trial was noted by BusinessWeek: "Early rounds of his deposition show him offering obfuscatory answers and saying 'I don't recall' so many times that even the presiding judge had to chuckle. Many of the technology chief's denials and pleas of ignorance have been directly refuted by prosecutors with snippets of emails Gates both sent and received."

https://en.wikipedia.org/wiki/United_States_v._Microsoft_Corp.

Judge Jackson ruled against Microsoft on November 5, 1999, stating that Microsoft executives had, according to him, "proved, time and time again, to be inaccurate, misleading, evasive, and transparently false ... Microsoft is a company with an institutional disdain for both the truth and for rules of law that lesser entities must respect. It is also a company whose senior management is not averse to offering specious testimony to support spurious defenses to claims of its wrongdoing."

This is a repeated theme with the uber-rich going back to the Rockefeller anti-trust trial in 1911 when Standard Oil was ordered to be broken up into 34 companies after decades of monopolizing the oil industry. John D. Rockefeller hired public relations wiz Ivy Ledbetter Lee to shine up his tarnished public image by filming Mr. Rockefeller playing croquet and hugging his grandkids. Bill Gates, like Rockefeller, created a public image as a charitable do-gooder who gives away millions to non-profits.

Ivy Ledbetter Lee, nicknamed "Poison Ivy" by his detractors, become one of the founding members of the Council on Foreign Relations, and also worked for the Nazi party in Germany, dispensing free advice to none other than Nazi propaganda minister Joseph Goebbels.

Bill Gates talks like Kermit the Frog, smiles like a harmless nerd and wears pink sweaters, but meanwhile, behind his carefully crafted image, he's sadistically murdering millions with his mass vaccine program, and getting richer and more powerful in the process.

America

Despite the glaring truth that the United States initiated 70 years of interventions, invasions and regime changes in scores of nations, many in our movement seem oblivious or unable to blame the "indispensable nation." America is like the beautiful, innocent girl-next-door who got addicted to heroin, became a prostitute, and still her neighbors say, "she was such a nice girl."

Some basic facts about the United States, or more accurately, we should say the American Empire: America has the largest GDP in the world and the largest military, with over 800 overseas bases. America owns 95 percent of the infrastructure of the internet as was shown in 2021, when the US shut down 30 Iranian national news websites for "disinformation."

https://www.presstv.ir/Detail/2021/06/25/660861/Seizure-of-regional-websites-not-free-speech

Americans own all the largest social media giants, such as Facebook, Twitter and YouTube who have been on a censorship purge for the last two years, deleting and indiscriminately banning thousands of accounts.

The United Nations was created by the United States with UN headquarters in New York on land donated by Nelson Rockefeller. The Rockefeller Foundation also was intimately connected to the World Health Organization and still is to this day: "The [Rockefeller Foundation] had enormous bearing on WHO, just as it did on the overall international health arena: WHO's very configuration was unthinkable without the [Foundation]."

https://www.academia.edu/67141292/
Backstage the relationship between the Rockefeller Foundation and the World Health Organization Part I 1940s 1960s

The two mega-corporations that are documented owning everything that breathes are BlackRock and Vanguard, both American companies. Without descending into America-bashing, we need to be aware of how far into the abyss things have gotten with the good 'ole USA. For a more sobering and detailed account of the downfall of America, check out Chris Hedges' scathing, albeit bleak book, written pre-pandemic. Things have only gotten worse.

https://www.amazon.com/America-Farewell-Tour-Chris-Hedges/dp/150115267X

At a book promoting event in Denver, Colorado in 2019, Hedges gave an hour-long presentation, at the end of which he concluded, "The only thing left for us to do is civil disobedience."

Atheism

Satan gets the blame for everything it seems. Christians are particularly adamant that the root of all evil is the devil, despite the famous verse that "the love of money is the root of all evil."

Jesus of Nazareth was wise to point out that the choice was between God and Money, not between God and Satan. *"No servant can be the slave of two masters; such a slave will hate one and love the other or will be loyal to one and despise the other. You cannot serve both God and money." --Luke 16:13*

If it's not Satan, then who is it?

In a materialistic society, when people have abandoned God, religion and spirituality in favor of science and technology, the only choice for a good life is piling up money and possessions. If there is no kingdom of heaven living within us, then we can't find happiness from within, only from the external, material world.

Atheism, materialism, secularism and humanism have infected the world on a scale never before imagined in history. Like a virus that spreads and infects everyone, the disease of materialism has caused more damage than anything else.

Materialism leads to totalitarian police states which in turn lead to world wars. It's that simple. Fascism, communism and materialistic capitalism all exist independently of belief in God, creation, spirituality, a Higher Power, an inner state of higher consciousness or the everywhere-present spirit that bathes our world in holy light.

Modern people erroneously believe we don't need God or spirituality; no matter what your view of the spiritual universe, we all need the inner life in order to survive and thrive as a species, as a biological race, and as spiritual beings. We are inwardly connected to an invisible, yet real spiritual universe and we all need to connect to the Source and Center of this spiritual universe.

The history of ALL totalitarian regimes includes persecution and/or control of religions. We have witnessed this over the last two years as churches, mosques, temples and synagogues were all shut down, with the explicit support of their leaders and membership.

I've Seen the Enemy and it's Us

Very few commentators in our society, or even from our Freedom Movement, accept any personal responsibility for the sins of the world. Most of us are looking for a scapegoat, someone to blame for all the problems of the world, but the truth is we are all members of society and we have all partnered to a lesser or greater degree to create the current mess we find ourselves in.

Even if we are ultimately successful in arresting and convicting all those who have orchestrated the plandemic, we still will not have solved the majority of our global problems. We still have enormous economic, political, technological, social and religious issues that are not going to simply go away just because Schwab and his crew of nut jobs are locked up. Nations still need to grapple with the general day-to-day challenges of running their economies and making sure their nations are moving in a positive direction. We have massive wealth inequality, resource challenges, religious differences, cultural and social problems and many, many more complex problems that confront our inter-connected, interdependent global world. Even with good people running the world, things will not be perfect or easy. Poverty, hunger and disease are not going to magically disappear if we lock up the bankers and other tyrants.

As a disclaimer, capitalism has done a lot of good for the world: Industrialization of our economies all over the world has resulted in an improved lifestyle for everyone. Having said that, it should also be noted that the inherent weakness of capitalism is that it is based on profit motive.

What we need is a service-based economy instead of a profit-based economy. This requires not a change in the system but a change in motivation, so that when people go to work in the morning, they go to serve the society instead of going to work to make a profit. That doesn't mean that people don't make a profit when they go to work it just means that the primary motivation changes to the higher values of social service, community building, neighborly goodwill and social brotherhood. The word service is derived from *serf* which referred to agriculture workers, originally a term for a guard or a shepherd.

Communism

It would not be fair to leave out communism, because a large percentage of our movement identifies communism as the ultimate enemy. The Marxist view of the world is that we are a two-tier class of capitalists and workers, and that history is the story of the struggle and animosity between the two groups. This is actually a cynical worldview. A much more universal worldview is that we are all brothers and sisters in a global family, not just brothers in solidarity because we belong to the same labor union. If we see the world as a global family, then everyone becomes, not just a citizen or a neighbor, but also our brother or sister. Then when we view people like Bill Gates or Klaus Schwab, we just see them as brothers who have lost their way and betrayed the family.

Instead of going to work to make a wage under the corporate agenda, we can go to work to serve our family, our neighbors, our society, our nation and our world. Then, we are working for the family business instead of for the corporate machine. This worldview leads to optimism and brotherly love.

Materialism and Marx's dialectical materialism reduces humans to the status of economic cogs in a dystopian capitalist machine. Materialism says that we are orphans in the universe without guardian or parent. A family without a father or mother or Creator could not exist. Biologically, all mammal life comes from the womb of a nurturing mother.

Marxist view of society is not necessarily wrong that we do not have classes, but in reality, we have many more than two classes. Western society is subdivided into the following classes:

1. The super-uber wealthy trillionaires. This would be a small handful of bankers and oil tycoons, the Rothschilds and Rockefellers.

2. The billionaire class. Currently there are an estimated 2668 billionaires in the world

3. The millionaire class

4. The middle class

5. The working class

6. The working poor

7. Homeless people

In the 36th annual Forbes list of the world's billionaires, the list included 2,668 billionaires with a total net wealth of $12.7 trillion, down 97 members from 2021.

There are currently 56.08 million adult millionaires in the world, with a total net worth of $191.6 trillion. They make for 1.1% of the population.

The top three countries that have the most millionaires are the US (39.1%), China (9.4%), and Japan (6.6%).
https://fortunly.com/statistics/millionaire-statistics/

Neither capitalism nor communism can save the world, nor can they provide enlightenment or raise our state of consciousness to a higher level. Well-applied capitalism may increase your bank account and lead to economic security, and add happiness and comfort to your life, but it won't heal our world, change the hearts of our political leaders or stop the elites from continuing their draconian agenda.

12 / Freedom Cells Revisited

We attended a Freedom Cell group recently in East Vancouver with over 25 people in attendance. There was lots of food and wine to go with the comradery of fellow freedom fighters.

The host asked us to hand over our phones after turning them off. It was mentioned that CSIS, assuming they were monitoring us, were already aware we were there because everyone had their phones on, so our GPS would have led them to the house. Someone else also chimed in, claiming CSIS, or any other bad actor could listen in to our conversation through a smart TV or via the SMART meter in the house.

Needless to say, paranoia took over and the host put all our phones in a big faraday bag and locked them in the closet anyway and moved on with the meeting. The main topic was escaping to Mexico. Not sure how it could be called a Freedom Cell if everybody was running away? Maybe it would have been better called an Escape Cell?

After the group talked for several minutes on the best way to get across the border without a vaxx pass, someone appropriately asked, "What would happen to Canada if all the Freedom Fighters moved to Mexico?" After a deafening silence, one of the members answered, "Canada would be lost."

After some heated debate, the host shut down the convo, and declared we all had a right to our opinions and we shouldn't look down on people if they want to flee to Mexico in search of greener pastures.

The truth is if we all leave the country, Trudeau and his WEF handlers would consolidate their power, and Canada would be turned into a techno-surveillance state overnight.

In order to be diligent, we should consider the possibility that Canada may be overrun by the WEF and we may be forced to flee. In the run up to WW2, the Nazis in Germany increasingly gained more and more power, and soon after consolidating their power, purged the nation of their enemies and started a horrific war. Without the contrarian voice of dissidents, a nation is doomed.

Hypothetically, if something like that happened to Canada, and we cannot rule out the possibility, even if it is just for the sake of discussion – if Canada was indeed lost, we would be forced to flee for our lives and that would mean heading for the American border, in order to make our way south to Mexico.

The only other options would be to find a ship heading east or south. Russia might be an option, in the event of things going totally sideways, but Russia does not look like a picnic nation to live in, especially if you do not speak the language. This is true of any nation we might think of escaping to. Starting a new life in a strange nation is not easy and most of us are in the over forty category.

Most of us, in the Freedom community, would rather die than take the experimental mRNA injection, so if the only option is leaving Canada, we would have to seriously consider starting over elsewhere.

There may be a positive outcome in this however. Stephen King's novel *The Stand*, written in 1978, arguably his epic masterpiece, is the story of a bioweapon that kills 99.4% of the world's population. Two groups of survivors emerge, one dominated by a sociopathic cowboy, Randall Flagg; and the other group follow a dream they all experience about a kind old grandmother that leads them to Boulder, Colorado. Flagg's group congregate in Las Vegas.

Whether this novel is prophetic, remains to be seen, though the possibility exists that the Freedom movement may be driven into one geographical location to fight a pitched battle with the elites. Currently, the Russians are discussing withdrawing from the WHO and the WTO, plus many other western organizations. They are creating their own trading network at the same time with other like-minded countries such as China, India and Brazil who are tired of US/NATO domination.

Alternatively, the Freedom Movement, who represent the new and better way, may create parallel societies within nations. The Godless Rulers can carry on, while the true Golden Rulers create their own new world. Those who live by the golden rule will eventually conquer the Earth, not by might nor by power but by the power of love with the inspiration of the original Source and Center of all the Universe.

Parallel Societies

There is a mild debate in the Freedom community over whether we should be confronting the system or whether we should just focus on building a new society and a new system. Many insist we need to create parallel structures and wait for the system to collapse. Others insist we need to fight through the legal/political system and reform from within.

Maybe the answer is both.

Much of our modern institutions are not broken, just in need of reform and restructuring. We also need new laws to prevent sociopaths from becoming entrenched in our political, economic and social systems. We need new institutions and new ways of doing things to adapt to our ever-changing modern world. We can't go back.

Canada is regularly placed on the top 10 best countries in the world to live in. Not perfect or utopia, but relative to the rest of the world, we have it pretty good here. Or we should say *had*. Our government has been infiltrated by the WEF, that much is confirmed. We need to get them out. Plain and simple. And they need to be replaced with trustworthy people who cannot be bought. That is our challenge.

13 / Echo Chambers

During the early days of the Freedom Movement, we witnessed the natural human reaction to government over-reach and systemic oppression. The original style of the protestors was likewise reactionary. Even the names and slogans that were chosen were symbolic of indignation and the sense of injustice of the oppressive mandates of our health official Bonnie Henry who ruled with an arbitrary, soft fascist fist.

Our movement sprang up spontaneously and organically, without plans, agendas or organization. It was just a happening. Psychologists have long studied how the influence of ideas and behaviors often spread spontaneously and unconsciously throughout a social group, society or nation. They generally call this *social contagion;* ironically, they study how movements spread contagiously, like a virus.

Usually they divide these up into categories of social, emotional, hysterical and echo contagion. For example, in reference to emotional contagion, when someone is in a good mood it puts others in a good mood, and vice versa, if someone is angry, negative or unhappy.

Because human beings are social creatures, we are easily influenced and controlled by the dominant idea, culture or attitude of the herd, and we are instinctively drawn to conformist behavior, whether we care to admit it or not. It causes human beings anxiety and/or cognitive dissonance when we deviate from the culturally accepted norms of our social group.

According to a recent study published in the National Institute of Health online journal, "Recent findings showed that users on Facebook tend to select information that adhere to their system of beliefs and to form polarized groups — i.e., echo chambers. Such a tendency dominates information cascades and might affect public debates on social relevant issues."

https://www.ncbi.nlm.nih.gov/pmc/articles/PMC5131349/

The study actually quotes a World Economic Forum article discussing echo chambers on social media and how difficult it is to control "disinformation." The author of the article stresses, "The problem is that while traditional media had editors, producers and other filters before information went public, individual publishing has no filter. You simply say what you want and put it out there."

https://www.weforum.org/agenda/2016/01/q-a-walter-quattrociocchi-digital-wildfires/

What is most revealing is the degree and extent of the WEF in their efforts to study and control "misinformation" and online rumors "about global conspiracies, chem-trails, UFOs, reptilians. One of the more publicized conspiracies is the link between vaccines and autism." The World Economic Forum lists digital misinformation as one of the main risks for modern society. The studies conclude, after massive and mind-numbing statistical analysis, that "conspiracy" Facebook groups primarily discuss four broad topics: environment (climate change, chemtrails, carbon tax), health (vaccines, side effects), diet, and geopolitics (Ukraine, NWO, Biden, Russia, China.)

Those who discuss geopolitics are the most engaged online and those who discuss diet are the least engaged in online Facebook conspiracy groups. In other words, those who study and understand the big picture of what the elites are trying to achieve on the global stage are the biggest threat online. They will have a very difficult time achieving their goals if their actions are exposed and their lies uncovered by those who clearly understand their geopolitical agenda.

https://arxiv.org/pdf/1504.05163.pdf

Furthermore, the WEF's 2022 Global Risk Assesment claims "that societal and environmental risks have worsened the most since the start of the pandemic, with "social cohesion erosion" and "livelihood crises" taking the top spots. Other risks identified as having worsened significantly are "debt crises", "cybersecurity failures", "digital inequality" and "backlash against science".

https://www3.weforum.org/docs/
WEF_The_Global_Risks_Report_2022.pdf

The WEF's analysis is so dispassionate and cold, considering its draconian attack on civil rights through the pandemic restrictions; the utter ruthlessness of their agenda is plain. They are intensely interested in how people form echo chambers because they want to eliminate all echo chambers except their own. They want a singular one-eyed narrative that all the world's citizens will follow; a one-world matrix of media-generated reality.

My Echo Chamber is Better Than Your Echo Chamber

In our media-dominated social matrix, we have entered a strange world of unreality where data has replaced truth and it has become a monetized commodity. We are in the Post-Truth Era.

The Freedom Community needs to become its own echo chamber in order to survive. We must make the Truth echo and reverberate around the world, until it resonates and causes a high frequency feedback loop that cannot be silenced. With the right frequency, earthquakes can be created and our Freedom Movement needs to discover and create the right frequency that the vaccinated and brainwashed ears will hear.

Unreality

In any pursuit of truth, whether it is a discussion of scientific truth about our physical world or a discussion of spiritual truth about the laws of the universe, the goal is to discover how physical or spiritual reality works. Without an understanding of reality, it is difficult for human beings to progress and evolve. Societies who accept a false reality, such as the society we currently live in, are in danger of becoming unreal.

Each person is unique and has a unique personality. We are like snowflakes, no two are ever alike. The range of personality is infinite and limitless. This is the divine stamp upon human beings and reveals that the universe is not just a mechanized machine of energy and matter. We are a personality-dominated universe.

Evil is only temporary because evil cannot exist in a perfect, eternal universe. Evil is created by the wrong choices of freewill creatures who abandon, whether consciously or unconsciously, the path of perfection and eternal destiny. A human being who persistently and consciously rejects the divine path risks going beyond the point of no return and becoming what we call a psychopath or sociopath – a wicked, evil person with no remorse, no conscience and no divine guidance. Without the active and ongoing guidance of the inner spirit, humanity is doomed.

Ministry of Truth

"Every record has been destroyed or falsified, every book rewritten, every picture has been repainted, every statue and street building has been renamed, every date has been altered. And the process is continuing day by day and minute by minute. History has stopped. Nothing exists except an endless present in which the Party is always right."

— George Orwell, *1984*

At the time of this writing, the Biden administration has literally created a Disinformation Governance Board to address the spread of what they refer to as "mis-, dis-, and malinformation." Mostly, it is created to run defense for the U.S./NATO proxy war in the Ukraine to bolster American support and counter any information that destroys their Russia-bad propaganda. Putin is vilified as a neo-Hitler, similar to previous campaigns against Saddam Hussein and Muammar Gaddafi.

When truth becomes a commodity that can be manipulated, bought and sold, a nation has begun a long, slow descent into the abyss.

The Rat Park Experiment

"We live in a world of hype and it is important not to get drawn into it. Our strongest weapon is the literal truth."

— Dr. Bruce Alexander

To continue our discussion of human socialization, we observe that the elites are psychologists. They study human behavior, and then they study the data collected in order to learn how to manipulate and control people. They do this because they are control freaks and they get a mental woody when they trigger people and make them jump. This gives them a feeling of superiority and self-worth, an ego-rush that they become addicted to. Ultimately, like any addictive drug, it will destroy them.

Addiction is a byproduct of a society experiencing a loss of connection, first of all to family and secondly to the community. Addiction and isolation go hand in hand. The greater the loss of connection, the greater the need for the individual to seek solace in drugs, alcohol, sex and power.

In 1978, Canadian psychologist Bruce K. Alexander, affiliated with Simon Fraser University, conducted an experiment with rats that became known as the *Rat Park Experiment*. He created a massive "rat park" with wheels and balls of yarn, plenty of space and lots of rats of opposite sex so their was ample mating opportunity for all the rats. He allowed the rats the option of choosing either a fresh water dispenser or a dispenser laced with liquid morphine.

Previous studies with rats and addiction created isolating environments where a single, solitary rat was given the option of water or morphine solution and the rat would always load himself up with drugs.

The Rat Park Experiment found, time after time, that if rats were given community and activity, they would choose the water over the morphine. Even rats who were addicted to morphine and then introduced to the Rat Park slowly and voluntarily went through withdrawals and gave up on the morphine solution.

https://www.amazon.ca/Globalization-Addiction-Study-Poverty-Spirit/dp/0199588716

The team concluded that drugs are not the cause of the addictions but rather the person's environment feeds the addiction. Isolated people exhibit feelings of loneliness, hopelessness and lack of control because of their poor living conditions and lack of connection to others. This results in dependance on substances. Normal, healthy environments give people the strength to resist addiction.

Professor Alexander spent a lifetime studying addiction and he is a staunch critic of the failed War on Drugs here in Vancouver, Canada where the Downtown Eastside has become progressively worse after decades of state-sponsored programs that have had no effect on stemming the flood of homelessness and opioid addiction. Last year in 2021, the level of deaths through overdose hit an all-time high after months of lockdown, masking, social-distancing. The B.C. Coroners Service reported 2,224 opioid deaths in 2021, a 26 per cent spike from 2020.

https://vancouversun.com/news/local-news/2021-bc-deadliest-year-in-opioid-overdose-crisis

The tragic casualties of lockdowns, masking, social distancing and isolating people are on stark display here in Vancouver. The streets of Hastings and Main are exploding with tents and broken people on a scale beyond anything ever seen here before.

The elites understand only too well the intended results of their lockdown policies. These crimes against humanity on a global scale are beyond anything in human history and the damage to our societies is only beginning to be felt.

Hierarchy of Needs

According to Maslow's Hierarchy of Needs, after the basic physiological and safety needs are met, a human beings needs belonging to feel fulfilled. The response to the supposed virus has been a direct assault on the needs for love, intimate relationship and friendship. Isolation is psychologically deadly for human beings. It wears us down and chips away at our inner self like nothing else. A recent study conducted in December 2020 discussed this issue: "Quarantine has been associated with increased rates of suicide, anger, acute stress disorder, depression and post-traumatic stress disorder, with symptoms continuing even years after quarantine ends."

https://www1.racgp.org.au/ajgp/2020/december/psychological-consequences-of-social-isolation-and/

To sum up, we having diverging forces at play over the last two years: Firstly, we have the stress and anxiety of the pandemic created by media fear-mongering, government overreach and draconian health mandates. Secondly, we have the opposing force of our Fringe Minority that the Empire has also inadvertently created by pushing us all together. We act as a direct counterweight to their actions. As Sir Isaac Newton famously postulated, *For every action, there is an equal but opposite reaction.*

The silver lining, only dimly seen at the moment, but sure to become brighter and brighter in the near future, is that the agenda and policies of the Empire are forcing our Freedom Community to bond together like never before. We are creating, unconsciously and organically, a tightly-knit community of like-minded, yet very diverse citizens who share common goals of liberating our nations from the yoke of totalitarian madness, and rebuilding our societies on firmer, more compassionate, democratic foundations.

14 / Humans Anonymous

"Abandon yourself to God as you understand God. Admit your faults to Him and to your fellows. Clear away the wreckage of your past. Give freely of what you find and join us. We shall be with you in the Fellowship of the Spirit, and you will surely meet some of us as you trudge the Road of Happy Destiny.
May God bless you and keep you—until then."
~ From Alcoholics Anonymous Big Book

There needs to be a fundamental shift in the collective conscience of the whole world. We, as a global family, need an intervention, whether divine or human, to break through the dysfunctional vicious cycle that has characterized the human race for most of our jaded past. Alcoholics often have to hit rock bottom before they realize they need to get help in order to change. Our entire planet needs an epic 12-step program where everyone stands up and admits they are powerless and the world has become unmanageable.

And just like alcoholics, who are notorious for their inability to face their problems, our planet is in denial. Wikipedia has this to say about denial:

In psychology, denialism is a person's choice to deny reality as a way to avoid a psychologically uncomfortable truth.

In psychoanalytic theory, denial is a defense mechanism in which a person is faced with a fact that is too uncomfortable to accept and rejects it instead, insisting that it is not true despite what may be overwhelming evidence. The concept of denial is important in twelve-step programs where the abandonment or reversal of denial that substance dependence is problematic forms the basis of the first, fourth, fifth, eighth and tenth steps.

https://en.wikipedia.org/wiki/Denial

And just like alcoholics, the truth is that the elites aren't really in control. They want to be in total control, but in fact, they are out of control, power-mad, wealthaholics that have been enabled by the rest of the co-dependent human race. Bullies need enablers to survive.

The Merriam-Webster dictionary gives this definition of co-dependency:

A psychological condition or a relationship in which a person manifesting low self-esteem and a strong desire for approval has an unhealthy attachment to another often controlling or manipulative person (such as a person with an addiction to alcohol or drugs)

broadly: dependence on the needs of or on control by another

Just look at the way the world fauns and adores sociopaths like Bill Gates, Elon Musk, Donald Trump and countless others. Hitler and the Nazis developed enough popular support to enable them to take power and steer Germany in the direction they wanted through a mix of propaganda, the personality cult of Hitler himself and open threats, very similar to how Bonnie Henry has conducted herself in the last two years.

Our whole planet needs a 12-step program similar to Alcoholics Anonymous, a plan of recovery to help us all overcome our addiction to money, power, sex, ambition and the selfish pursuit of happiness without consideration for others. We could call it Humans Anonymous. Though it may seem comical, attendees at Humans Anonymous could stand up and introduce themselves: "Hello, my name is Dave and I am a human."

The first step needs to happen first.

1. We admitted we were powerless over our planet — that our lives and our world has become unmanageable.

The second step of the global 12-step program is for the world to *"come to realize that a Power great than ourselves can restore us to sanity."*

And the third step is for the whole world *to collectively decide to turn our will and our planet over to the care of God as we have come to understand him.*

To summarize:

1. We admitted we were powerless over our planet — that our lives and our world has become unmanageable.

2. Came to believe that a Source greater than ourselves could restore us to sanity.

3. Made a decision to turn our will and our planet over to the care of God as we understood him.

And a special note to the last phrase in Step 3: *God as we understood him.* It is important for everyone, not only in our Freedom Movement but also for the rest of the world, to know that everyone is at different stages in their spiritual walk and has a different, often personal understanding of God.

12-Step Recovery Program for Humans

1. We admitted we were powerless over our planet — that our lives and our world has become unmanageable.

2. Came to believe that a Source greater than ourselves could restore us to sanity.

3. Made a decision to turn our will and our planet over to the care of God as we understood him.

4. Made a searching and fearless moral inventory of our planet.

5. Admitted to God, to ourselves, and to other human beings the exact nature of our wrongs.

6. Were entirely ready to have God remove all these defects of character from our planet.

7. Humbly asked him to remove our shortcomings.

8. Made a list of all human beings we had harmed, and became willing to make amends to them all.

9. Made direct amends to such human beings wherever possible, except when to do so would injure them or others.

10. Continued to take personal inventory and when we were wrong promptly admitted it.

11. Sought through prayer and meditation to improve our conscious contact with God as we understood him, praying only for knowledge of his will for Earth and the power to carry that out.

12. Having had a spiritual awakening as the result of these 12-Steps, we tried to carry this message to other human beings, and to practice these principles in all our affairs.

15 / Fringe Benefits for the Fringe Minority

"I am a Canadian. Canada has been the inspiration of my life. I have before me as a pillar of fire by night and as a pillar of cloud by day a policy of true Canadianism, of moderation, of conciliation."

– Wilfred Laurier

Though it is an often repeated cliché, there is always a silver lining in the clouds, and our movement has a multitude of silver linings for those with eyes to see. If the hidden secrets of our movement are let out of the bag, many more will join our common cause when they learn of how beneficial getting involved can be for everyone.

The movement itself can be a vehicle for many to experience personal growth, healing and recovery from childhood and adulthood trauma. Fighting for freedom is a learning curve for all of us, and the movement can be an accelerator of personal growth. Here is a brief list of the many Fringe Benefits for the Fringe Minority.

1. Learning to let go

People in our movement need to let go of the attachments to the things that got us into this mess in the first place. Attachment to possessions, ambition, sex, alcohol, drugs and money for starters.

2. Inner Healing

Our society has issues, and that would be an understatement. We all have been damaged by family, friends, relationships and the constant negativity of our society. Crisis pushes us inward where we are forced to deal with our inner issues. We carry our "pain body" around with us every day, the accumulated pains of a lifetime. Going inward is a healing experience.

3. Personal Development

There are so many avenues now to get involved with and so many emerging groups to join, that the door is wide open for people to expand their skills and abilities or develop new skills and abilities. We are pioneers of a new and better world and this leads to opportunities for tremendous personal growth.

4. Becoming a politician

Many have become candidates and run for office in the PPC, MLA's or local school boards, people who never even considered running for public office are now doing it. We need to get involved with the political process in order to take back our country.

5. Being a Pioneer

We are part of a fledgling movement that is local, provincial, national and international. We are heading into unknown territory, going where "no man has gone before." It is an adventure of a lifetime, a privileged time not only to be alive, but also to have the opportunity to take part in the greatest epoch in human history. We are creating a new "Wild Wild West" at the same time as the Empire of Greed is collapsing.

6. Starting a New Thing

It is always better to be part of a movement that is on the upswing, where the opportunity is present to start something new, that has not been done before. The time for startup companies is wide open. We need a new economy and new business models that are off the grid and not part of the matrix, new ways and new business models.

7. Spiritual Growth

Our world is suffering from chronic spiritual apathy and needs a new injection of spiritual enthusiasm. The door is wide open for motivated and dynamic believers to start new spiritual groups and serve others. Service to others causes us to grow and mature spiritually. We can become better people and grow closer to God and become more Godlike.

8. New friends and family

Most of us have witnessed our social circle explode in the last two years. Ironically, while the rest of the world sat at home, afraid to go out because of the mythologized virus, our community got together more than ever. We had parties and get togethers, endless rallies, events, workshops, potluck dinners, cell groups and picnics. It was epic. And the party is just getting started.

Epilogue / The Road Ahead

Anyone who has spent some time studying the world's religions, and more specifically studying the lives of the leaders of those religions, is aware that those leaders share commonalities and similar experiences in their lives.

Jesus of Nazareth, Siddhartha Gautama (Buddha,) Nanak (Sikh founder) all gave up everything in their pursuit of the will of God, enlightenment and the meaning of life.

A truly spiritual person is characterized by a loss of interest in the things that the majority of people spend their lives chasing after such as money, wealth, possessions, sex, fame, career and social recognition. They also exhibit a lack of interest in alcohol, drugs and other addictions.

Those who are truly committed to our Freedom movement are similarly going down a positive spiritual path, whether they are conscious of it or not.

This author first spoke to Dr. Charles Hoffe on the phone as he was driving up to his cabin in northern BC. At that time he had lost his practice in Lytton, he had been banned from the emergency room which was half of his income and then the town of Lytton burned to the ground. His wife and children had rejected him due to his passion for Christianity. Several months later he was the guest speaker at a local church in White Rock.

He was practically in tears at several points in his speech which was more of a sermon than a speech. In some ways at that moment, he became the movements' Luke, the physician turned apostle who wrote one of the four gospels and the book of Acts.

Many people in the movement including this author have lost their jobs for either refusing to wear the mask or refusing to be vaccinated. This is a very difficult decision to make for some people but for others there was no decision really, because they would rather die than be injected with an evil toxic waste injection. Bill Gates and the World Health Organization along with the WEF and Klaus Schwab forced us to draw a line in the sand. Like Gandalf in the scene in The Lord of the Rings when he is confronting the Balrog, we have declared "You shall not pass!"

The elites who run the Empire of Evil appear on the world stage as surreal villains in an apocalyptic movie. Klaus Schwab talks like a character from a Marvel Comics sequel. Reality is truly stranger than fiction.

From the universe perspective, there are no good people or bad people, there are just people who take the good road and others who take the bad road. The way to eternity, enlightenment, awakening and salvation is not always easy and sometimes offers no immediate reward.

As we discussed in a previous chapter there are Fringe Benefits for the Fringe Minority and our choice to fight for freedom leads to increased opportunity for spiritual at-one-ment with the universe. We can count on the following spiritual benefits if we continue down the good path:

- Maturity
- Spiritual growth
- Increased happiness
- Decreasing addiction
- Decreasing disputes with others
- Better quality friendships and relationships
- A sense of purpose and meaning
- Greater responsibility to others
- Greater understanding of the world

Jesus of Nazareth's Program for Activists

Jesus of Nazareth taught a radical plan of action for those persecuted by governments. He encouraged his followers to pray, especially for those who persecuted them, and to love their enemies. This is not an easy task when our enemies hate us, take away our rights and force people to be injected with toxic chemicals.

Most of us in our Freedom Movement in Canada dislike Justin Trudeau with a passion and we ridicule him constantly on social media. Can we win over our enemies with love? Are they even redeemable people? Klaus Schwab is about as lovable as a crocodile but can we love him and will it matter?

Personally, Schwab would be a whole lot more lovable if he was locked up in a dungeon somewhere. Maybe we could visit him and throw some salt on his wounds. Jesus of Nazareth, however, asked that his enemies be forgiven when he was being tortured to death because "they know not what they do." Do the elites really know what they are doing? Are they so blind to themselves? Your guess is as good as anyone's.

The Weapons of Our Warfare

The weapons of our warfare are words, the written and spoken word. The words we speak from the microphone at rallies and protests, the words we speak from the megaphone when we march in solidarity down the streets of our cities. The words we type into our keyboards on Facebook and Twitter, ridiculing our government and lying media when they spew their propaganda and lies. The words we write on petitions, notices of liability and lawsuits that our activists, representatives and lawyers use to challenge our governments, education and judicial system. The words we use to persuade our family and friends, to gently wake them up, to shake them in their slumber and apathy.

The weapons of our warfare are printed on stickers that are posted on bus stop shelters, street lights, bathroom stalls and mailboxes. Our weapons are the words spoken by our independent journalists who challenge their narrative, and provide an alternative viewpoint to the singularity of the mainstream media who have prostituted themselves to the government and their WEF masters.

The weapons of our warfare are spoken softly, whispered under our breath when we awaken from troubled sleep and disturbing dreams of apocalypse, darkness and fright. The weapons of our warfare are thundered from portable sound systems, spoken by passionate citizens, both men and women standing in the rain and the cold in the box of pickup trucks on the streets of our cities.

The weapons of our warfare are words spoken in thousands upon thousands of video posts on Tiktok, Instagram, YouTube, Rumble, Facebook, Twitter and Telegram. Our weapons are memes lampooning the Justin Trudeaus, Boris Johnsons and Joe Bidens of the world, exposing the evil of Klaus Schwab, Bill Gates, the World Health Organization, the WEF and the Davos billionaires who gather yearly to plot destruction and domination.

The weapons of our warfare are the words spoken by doctors, nurses and medical scientists who warned the population about the MRNA experimental injections. They spoke publicly and privately, in newspapers and books, in peer reviewed articles and at our demonstrations. They showed the data and explained the science, and predicted the outcome of vaccine injuries and death.

And finally, the supreme weapon of our warfare are the unspoken words we express in our deepest dreams and highest ideals of human compassion and freedom. It is the words we speak in fervent prayer to the Source and Center of the Universe, our inspiration and guide through these troubled times.

Manufactured by Amazon.ca
Bolton, ON